FOURTH EDITION

WORLD LINK INTRO

DEVELOPING ENGLISH FLUENCY

NANCY DOUGLAS
JAMES R. MORGAN

NATIONAL
GEOGRAPHIC
LEARNING

ustralia · Brazil · Canada · Mexico · Singapore · United Kingdom · United States

NATIONAL GEOGRAPHIC
LEARNING

National Geographic Learning,
a Cengage Company

World Link Level Intro: Developing English Fluency,
Fourth Edition

Publisher: Sherrise Roehr

Executive Editor: Sarah Kenney

Managing Editor: Claudi Mimó

Director of Global Marketing: Ian Martin

Heads of Regional Marketing:
  Charlotte Ellis (Europe, Middle East and Africa)
  Irina Pereyra (Latin America)

Senior Product Marketing Manager:
  Caitlin Thomas

Content Project Manager: Beth Houston

Media Researcher: Stephanie Eenigenburg

Cover/Text Design: Lisa Trager

Art Director: Brenda Carmichael

Operations Support: Hayley Chwazik-Gee,
  Avi Mednick, Katie Lee

Manufacturing Planner: Mary Beth Hennebury

Composition: MPS North America LLC

For permission to use material from this text or product,
submit all requests online at **cengage.com/permissions**
Further permissions questions can be emailed to
permissionrequest@cengage.com

Student's Book
ISBN: 978-0-357-50209-9
Student's Book + My World Link Online:
ISBN: 978-0-357-50210-5

National Geographic Learning
200 Pier 4 Boulevard
Boston, MA 02210
USA

Locate your local office at **international.cengage.com/region**

Visit National Geographic Learning online at **ELTNGL.com**
Visit our corporate website at **www.cengage.com**

Printed in Mexico
Print Number: 01 Print Year: 2021

Acknowledgments

Thank you to the educators who provided invaluable feedback throughout the development of the *World Link* series:

Asia

Michael Jake Arcilla, Aii Language Center, Phnom Penh; Fintan Brennan, Meisei University, Tokyo; Tyler Burden, Meisei University, Tokyo; Catherine Cheetham, Tokai University, Tokyo; Will Fan, Xiamen Wanda, Xiamen; Mark Firth, Oberlin University, Machida; Hiroshi Fukuda, Jumonji University, Niiza; Thomas Goetz, Hokusei Gakuen University, Sapporo; Helen Hanae, Reitaku University, Kashiwa; Louis Liu, Meten English, Shenzen; Shaun McLewin, Hanseo University, Seosan; Raymond Monk, Jr., Meten English, Dalian; Donald Patterson, Seirei Christopher University, Hamamatsu City; Mongkol Sodachan, Rangsit University, Pathum Thani; Robert Wright, Meten English, Chengdu; Elvira Wu, Meten English, Quanzhou; I-Cheng Wu, Southern Taiwan University of Science and Technology, Tainan City; Xie Yu, SFLEP, Shanghai; Vince Zhang, Thinktown, Hangzhou; Vivi Zhang, Xiamen Wanda, Xiamen

Latin America

Anthony Acevedo, ICPNA, Lima; Jorge Aguilar, Centro de Estudios de Idiomas UAS, Culiacan; Lidia Stella Aja, Centro Cultural Colombo Americano, Cali; Ana Laura Alferez, Instituto Domingo Savio, Mexico City; Lúcia Rodrigues Alves, Seven, Sao Paulo; Alessandra Atarcsay, WOWL Education, Rio de Janeiro; Isabella Campos Alvim, IBEU Copacabana, Rio de Janeiro; Ana Berg, Ana Berg EFL School, Rio de Janeiro; Raul Billini, Santo Domingo; Isabela Villas Boas, Casa Thomas Jefferson, Brasilia; Lourdes Camarillo, Escuela Bancaria Comercial, Mexico City; Cinthia Castañeda, Centro de Idiomas, Coatzacoalcos; Enrique Chapuz, Universidad Veracruzana, Coatzacoalcos; Giseh Cuesta, MESCyT, Mexico City; Carlos Fernández, ICPNA, Lima; Vania Furtado, IBEU Copacabana, Rio de Janeiro; Mariana Garcia, BUAP, Puebla; Jeanette Bravo Garonce, IPA Idiomas, Brasilia; Luiz Henrique Bravo Garonce, IPA Idiomas, Brasilia; Fily Hernandez, Universidad Veracruzana, Coatzacoalcos; Manuel Hidalgo Iglesias, Escuela Bancaria Comercial, Mexico City; Dafna Ilian, ESIME, Azcapotzalco; Rubén Jacome, Universidad Veracruzana, Coatzacoalcos; Beatriz Jorge, Alumni, Sao Paulo; Gledis Libert, ICDA, Santo Domingo; Rocio Liceaga, International House, Mexico City; Elizabeth Palacios, ICPNA, Lima; Emeli Borges Pereira Luz, UNICAMPI, Sao Paulo; Patricia McKay, CELLEP, Sao Paulo; Victor Hugo Medina, Cultura Inglesa Minas Gerais, Belo Horizonte; Maria Helena Meyes, ACBEU, Salvador; Isaias Pacheco, Universidad Veracruzana, Coatzacoalcos; Miguel Rodriguez, BUAP, Puebla; Nelly Romero, ICPNA, Lima; Yesenia Ruvalcaba, Universidad de Guadalajara, Guadalajara; Eva Sanchez, BUAP, Puebla; Marina Sánchez, Instituto Domingo Savio, Mexico City; Thais Scharfenberg, Centro Europeu, Curitiba; Pilar Sotelo, ICPNA, Lima; Rubén Uceta, Centro Cultural Domínico Americano, Santiago De Los Caballeros; Italia Vergara, American English Overseas Center, Panama City; Maria Victoria Guinle Vivacqua, UNICAMP, Sao Paulo

United States and Canada

Bobbi Plante, Manitoba Institute of Trades and Technology, Winnipeg; Richard McDorman, Language On Schools, Miami, FL; Luba Nesteroba, Bilingual Education Institute, Houston, TX; Tracey Partin, Valencia College, Orlando, FL

SCOPE AND SEQUENCE

REAL WORLD LINK 1 Big City or Small Town? p. 44

REAL WORLD LINK 2 My Favorite Place to Eat p. 88

PRONUNCIATION	SPEAKING	READING	WRITING	ACTIVE ENGLISH	LISTENING AND READING SKILLS	GLOBAL VOICES
Contractions with *be* p. 6	Introducing yourself p. 6	Your Photo, Your Story p. 10	Write about your favorites p. 14	Provide personal information and interview classmates p. 8 Ask about favorites p. 14	Listen for numbers p. 5 Infer information p. 11 Listen for details p. 12	Nice to Meet You p. 15
Stressed syllables p. 18	Asking where someone is from p. 20	A Great Place to Visit p. 24	Write about a vacation p. 28	Play a board game about places and nationalities p. 22 Interview classmates about vacation spots p. 28	Listen for confirmation p. 19 Read for details p. 25 Listen for details p. 26	Andrés Ruzo: Map My Family p. 29
Plural endings p. 35	Giving and replying to thanks p. 34	Who Is Marie Kondo? p. 38	Write about objects in a room p. 42	Role play about giving and receiving gifts p. 36 Ask for and give advice about cleaning a room p. 42	Listen for details p. 33 Scan for information p. 38 Listen for the main idea p. 40	What's Your Favorite Gadget? p. 43
Combining words with *how* p. 50	Greeting people and asking how they are p. 50	Popular Online Classes p. 54	Fill out a questionnaire p. 58	Play charades p. 52 Interview classmates p. 58	Listen for specific information p. 49 Infer information p. 55 Listen for specific information p. 56	Voices from Chicago p. 59
And p. 63	Talking about likes and dislikes p. 64	Two Powerful Foods p. 68	Write about a favorite food p. 72	Plan a dinner party p. 66 Talk about a favorite food p. 72	Listen for details p. 63 Take notes p. 69 Predict p. 70	What to Eat in Peru p. 73
Possessive *'s* p. 79	Talking about age p. 78	Time to Get Married? p. 82	Write about relationship norms and preferences p. 86	Take a quiz about numbers and family p. 80 Take a relationship survey p. 86	Listen for details p. 77 Skim for the gist p. 83 Listen for details p. 84	All in the Family p. 87

SCOPE AND SEQUENCE

1

INTRODUCTIONS

LOOK AT THE PHOTO. COMPLETE 1 AND 2.

1. The people are ____.

   a. in class

   b. at a party

   c. at home

2. Match a conversation with the man and woman.

   a. –Hi. I'm Gabe.

     –My name is Elena.

   b. –Hello. I'm Ms. Medina, the teacher.

     –Good morning. My name is Gabe.

WARM-UP VIDEO

A Watch the video. Then circle **T** for *true* or **F** for *false*.

   1. Carlos is a student.   **T F**

   2. Carlos says *hi* to Ana.   **T F**

   3. Ana is a teacher.   **T F**

B Watch the video again. Say the sentences aloud as you watch.

C Watch one more time. Match the correct answers to complete the conversation on screen.

   1. _____   a. She's a student.

   2. _____   b. See you!

   3. _____   c. Hi!

   4. _____   d. Bye!

   5. _____   e. Hello!

   6. _____   f. He's a student.

D Now say *hi* and *bye* to a partner.

E What are other ways to say *hi* and *bye*?

People dance at
a silent disco.

GOALS

Lesson A
/ Introduce yourself and spell your name
/ Say phone numbers and email addresses

Lesson B
/ Talk about your favorites
/ Ask about a person's interests

Mei-Li

Lucas

Alberto

Noor

VOCABULARY

A Say the letters with your teacher.

A B C D E F G H I J K L M N O P Q R S T U V W X Y Z

B Say the letters with a partner. Then change roles and repeat.

Student A: Say A–M.

Student B: Say N–Z.

C Look at the photos above. Then listen. Write the last names. 🎧 2

First name	Last name
Mei-Li	
Alberto	
Lucas	
Noor	

D Check answers in **C** with a partner.

USEFUL EXPRESSION
Can you repeat that, please?

E Work with a partner.

1. **Student A:** Spell your first and last name.
2. **Student B:** Write your partner's name.
3. Change roles and repeat.

❝ My first name is
T-O-M-A-S.

Can you repeat
that, please? ❞

❝ Sure. T-O-M . . .

LISTENING

A Say the words in the Word Bank with your teacher.

B Matt is a teacher. He is meeting the students. Listen. Write the last name and nicknames. 🎧 3

WORD BANK

Numbers		Email addresses
0 zero*	6 six	@ = at
1 one	7 seven	.com = dot com
2 two	8 eight	.edu = dot e-d-u
3 three	9 nine	
4 four	10 ten	
5 five		

*For *zero*, say *oh* in a phone number.

First name	Last name	Nickname*	@ Email address	☎ Phone number
Matt			Matt._____@_____	(____) _____ - _____
Mei-Li	Yang		_____@easypost _____	(472) _____ - _____
Alberto	Cruz		AlbertoC@mylink _____	(____) _____ - _____

*nickname = a short or different name from your first name

C **Listen for numbers.** Listen again. Write the email addresses and phone numbers. 🎧 4

ℹ️ In English, people say each number in a phone number (4-7-2) 6-7-7 . . .

D Say the names, email addresses, and phone numbers in the chart.

E Write your information in the chart. The email address and phone number can be real or invented. Then tell a partner: *My . . . is . . .*

USEFUL EXPRESSION
Can you spell that, please?

❝ My email address is . . .

Can you spell that, please? ❞

Students say *hi* outside of school.

SOMEWHERE, SOMETHING INCREDIBLE IS WAITING TO BE KNOWN

SPEAKING

A Read and listen to the conversation. 🎧5

Maya: Hi, my name is Maya. What's your name?

Antonio: Hi, Maya. I'm Antonio.

Maya: Nice to meet you, Antonio.

Antonio: It's nice to meet you, too.

Two people meet and shake hands.

B PRONUNCIATION: Contractions with *be* Listen and repeat. 🎧6

1. What is ➜ What's ➜ What's your name?
2. I am ➜ I'm ➜ I'm Antonio.
3. It is ➜ It's ➜ It's nice to meet you.

C Practice the conversation in **A**.

D Practice the conversation in **A** again. Use your names.

E Meet six classmates. Use the Speaking Strategy. Write the names.

1. _____
2. _____
3. _____
4. _____
5. _____
6. _____

> **SPEAKING STRATEGY** 🎧7
>
> **Introducing Yourself**
> Hi. What's your name?
>   My name is . . . / I'm . . .
> (It's) nice to meet you.
>   (It's) nice to meet you, too.

GRAMMAR

A   Look at the chart.

1. Say the sentences with your teacher.
2. Say the words in **bold** only.
3. Complete the chart on the right.

> *I'm . . . my,*
> *you're . . . your*

SUBJECT PRONOUNS AND POSSESSIVE ADJECTIVES WITH *BE*					
I'm	a student.	**My**	name	**is**	Antonio.
You're		**Your**			Maya.
He's		**His**			Lucas.
She's		**Her**			Noor.
They're	students.	**Their**	names	**are**	Mei and Beto.

SAME SOUND DIFFERENT MEANING	
you're	
they're	

B   Read the Unit 1, Lesson A Grammar Reference in the appendix. Complete the exercises.

C   Look at the pictures. Then play the game with your class. How far can you go?

My name is Rina. I'm a student.

Your name is Rina, You're a student. My name is Lucas. I'm a student.

Her name is Rina. She's a student. Your name is Lucas. You're a student. My name is Jen. I'm a student.

D   Play again. This time, use numbers 1–9 and *he*, *his*, *she*, and *her*.

My name is Rina. I'm a student. My number is 8.

Her name is Rina. She's a student. Her number is 8. My name is Lucas. I'm a student. My number is 3.

Her name is Rina. She's a student. Her number is 8. His name is Lucas. He's a student. His number is 3. My name is Jen...

ACTIVE ENGLISH Try it out!

A Look at the answers. Write the questions.

1. What's _____?
   My name is Alma Valdez.

2. _____?
   My email address is avaldez@eazypost.com.

3. _____?
   It's (399) 555-7061.

B Imagine you are a new student. Think of a new name, phone number, and email address. Complete the information.

_____   _____
Last name   First name

(613)_____   _____
Phone number   Email address

C Meet four students. Write their information below. Use your "new" information from **B**.

Student 1	Student 2
Last name:	Last name:
First name:	First name:
Phone number:	Phone number:
Email address:	Email address:

Student 3	Student 4
Last name:	Last name:
First name:	First name:
Phone number:	Phone number:
Email address:	Email address:

1A GOALS   Now I can . . .

Introduce myself and spell my name _____

Say phone numbers and email addresses _____

1. Yes, I can.
2. Mostly, yes.
3. Not yet.

VOCABULARY

WORD BANK
Music

🎻 classical

🕺 dance

🎤 hip-hop / rap

📻 pop

Sports

⚾ baseball

🏀 basketball

⚽ soccer

🏊 swimming

A Look at the Word Bank.

1. Say the words with your teacher.

2. Think of two other types of music and sports. Tell the class.

B Su-Min is a student. Read about her favorite things. Complete 1–6 with an answer (a–f). Then check answers with a partner.

a. swimming	d. FC Barcelona
b. the new *Spider-Man* film	e. ~~Top Chef~~
c. dance	f. BTS (the K-Pop group)

Right now, her **favorite** . . .

1. **TV show** is ___e___.

2. kind of **music** is _____ music.

3. **singer** or **band** is _____.

4. **sport** is _____.

5. **sports team** or **player** is _____.

6. **movie** is _____.

C Tell a partner about your favorites.

Right now, my favorite . . .

1. TV show is _____.

2. kind of music is _____.

3. singer or band is _____.

4. sport is _____.

5. sports team or player is _____.

6. movie is _____.

> 66 Right now, my favorite TV show is . . .
>
> I'm into that show, too. 99

ℹ️ You can also say **be into**: *My favorite TV show is . . . = I'm into that show.*

D Tell a new person about your partner's answers in **C**.

> 66 My partner is Ruben. His favorite kind of music is . . .

Swimming at sunset

YOUR PHOTO, YOUR STORY

The photos on this page are personal portraits. A personal portrait is a kind of photo. It shows something important about you. Maybe Manchester United is your favorite soccer team. Maybe you are a student at a famous university. Maybe you are a singer in a band. A personal portrait is a photo of you. It also tells a story about you. 🎧 8

❶ Mikhail Vasilev is into _____.
It's his favorite _____.

② **Jessica Chege is a university student. She's interested in _____ and probably _____.**

The <u>underlined letters</u> in the words above make the same sound.

1. Say the words with your teacher.

2. Look up the words in your dictionary.

B Read. Complete the sentence with the correct answer(s).

A personal portrait is a ____.

a. kind of photo   c. picture of a famous person

b. soccer team   d. story about you

C Look at the photos. Complete the sentences about the people with words from the box. Two words are extra.

computers	science	sport
hip-hop	skateboarding	swimming

D **Infer information.** What are Mikhail and Jessica into? Tell a partner.

      ❝ He's into . . .

E Take your own personal portrait.

1. Write a sentence about you and one of your favorites.

2. Take a photo. In the photo, show the idea in your sentence.

      ❝ You're into . . .

            Yes, it's my favorite . . . ❞

F Work with a partner.

1. Student A: Show a partner your photo, not your sentence.

    Student B: Make a sentence about Student A's photo.

2. Change roles and repeat.

G Repeat **F** with three more people. Which photos are your favorites?

LISTENING

A Point to a photo. Tell a partner about it. Use a sentence in the box.
Take turns.

> It's a reality show.   It's a scary show.   It's a soccer game.

B **Listen for details.** Listen to a man and woman talk about TV shows.
Number each show (1, 2, or 3) as they talk about it.

C **Infer.** Listen again. Which show do they watch?
Write the number. _____

D Do people watch shows like this in your country?
What other shows are popular in your country? Tell a partner.

> " Soccer is popular.
>
> . . . is also popular. "

GRAMMAR

A Read the Unit 1, Lesson B Grammar Reference in the appendix. Complete the exercises. Then do the exercises below.

YES / NO QUESTIONS WITH BE			SHORT ANSWERS	
Be	Pronoun		Affirmative	Negative
Am	I	in this class?	Yes, you **are**.	No, you're **not**. / No, you **aren't**.
Are	you	a student?	Yes, I **am**.	No, I'm **not**.
Is	he / she		Yes, he / she **is**.	No, he's **not**. / No, she **isn't**.
Is	it	your favorite team?	Yes, it **is**.	No, it's **not**. / No, it **isn't**.
Are	they	pop singers?	Yes, they **are**.	No, they're **not**. / No, they **aren't**.

B Complete the conversations. Then practice them with a partner.

1. **A:** _____Are you_____ a student?

   B: Yes, _____.

2. **A:** _____ English your native language?

   B: No, _____.

3. **A:** _____ from here?

   B: No, _____. I'm from Mexico City.

4. **A:** _____ Cristiano Ronaldo your favorite soccer player?

   B: No, _____. I'm not into soccer.

5. **A:** _____ Lin-Manuel Miranda your favorite singer?

   B: Yes, _____. His music is great.

6. **A:** _____ friends with anyone from the US?

   B: Yes, _____. My friend Adam is from New York.

C Ask a partner the six questions in **B**. This time, talk about yourselves.

> 66 Are you a student?
> Yes, I am. 99

> 66 Is Lin-Manuel Miranda your favorite singer?
> No, he isn't. My favorite is . . . 99

Lin-Manuel Miranda performs in his musical *Hamilton*.

Star Wars: The Rise
of Skywalker

ACTIVE ENGLISH Try it out!

A WRITING Take four small pieces of paper. Write a sentence on each paper
about a favorite . . .

| singer or band | sport or video game | TV show or movie | website or podcast |

My favorite movie is *Star Wars: The Rise of Skywalker*.

B Give one sentence from **A** to your teacher.

C Your teacher will give you a classmate's sentence. Ask your classmates
Yes / No questions. Find the writer of the sentence.

" Is *Star Wars* your
favorite movie?

No, it's not. "

Yes, it is! It's
my sentence. "

D Repeat **C** with a different sentence.

1B GOALS Now I can . . .

Talk about my favorites ____

Ask about a person's interests ____

1. Yes, I can.
2. Mostly, yes.
3. Not yet.

GLOBAL VOICES

A   Look at the names in the chart. Then watch the video. Don't write anything.

	First name	Last name	Nickname	Favorites
1	Fabrizio	Riccadeli		
2	Vera			
3	Lissette			
4	Herman	Van der Muellen	The	
5	Gina			
6	Laura			
7	Abel			

WORD BANK

Beijing, China
Florence, Italy

B   Watch again. Write a last name or nickname in **A**.

C   Watch Lissette and Abel again. What are they into? Write the answers (a–e) in the chart. Two answers are extra.

   a. hip-hop   **b.** salsa music   **c.** reggaeton   **d.** basketball   **e.** soccer

D   Ask and answer the questions with a partner.

Student A: Ask questions 1–4.   **Student B:** Ask questions 5–8.

" Is he from China?

No, he isn't. He's . . . "

1. Fabrizio: Is he from China?

2. Vera: Can you spell her last name?

3. Lissette: Is her nickname *Lisa*? Is she into hip-hop?

4. Chris: Is *Chris* his first name?

5. Herman: What's his nickname? Can you spell it?

6. Gina: Can you spell her last name?

7. Laura: Is her last name *Perez?* Can you spell her last name?

8. Abel: Is he into salsa? Is his favorite sport basketball?

The Bund, Shanghai, China

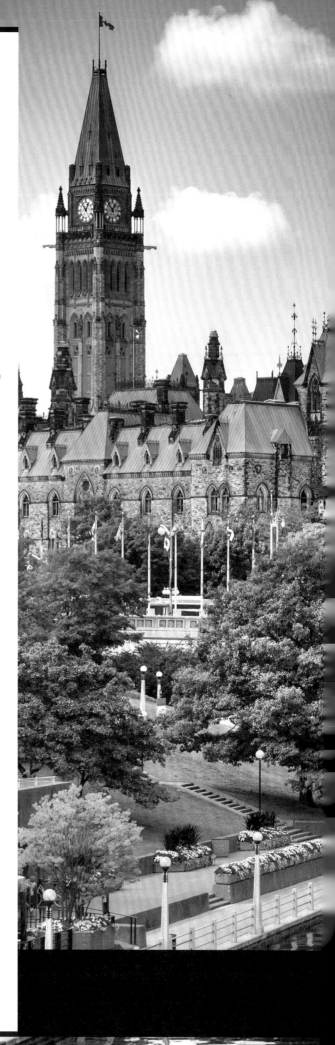

2

COUNTRIES

LOOK AT THE PHOTO. ANSWER THE QUESTIONS.

1. Ottawa is the capital of Canada. What is the capital city of your country?
2. There are many tourists in Ottawa. Are there many tourists in your city?

WARM-UP VIDEO

A Listen. Say each country after the speaker. 🎧10

☐ France   ☐ Peru   ☐ Thailand

☐ Jordan   ☐ Russia   ☐ Turkey

B Watch the video. Check (✓) the countries in **A** that you see in the video. One is extra.

C Watch again. Say three other countries in the video. Tell a partner.

D Listen. Say each city after the speaker. 🎧11

Bangkok	Istanbul
Cusco	La Paz
Fes	New York
Granada	Paris

E Do you know the cities and their countries? Guess. Then watch the video and match them.

1. Paris   a. Bolivia
2. Granada   b. France
3. Istanbul   c. Morocco
4. La Paz   d. Peru
5. Fes   e. Spain
6. New York   f. Thailand
7. Cusco   g. Turkey
8. Bangkok   h. USA

F Which place in the video is your favorite? Tell a partner.

The Parliament building in Ottawa, the capital city of Canada.

GOALS

Lesson A
/ Name countries and nationalities
/ Ask where someone is from

Lesson B
/ Talk about a city
/ Describe a good vacation place

A woman carrying the Swiss flag at the Olympic Games.

VOCABULARY

A PRONUNCIATION: Stressed syllables Listen and repeat. Say the countries and nationalities in the chart. 🎧12

B PRONUNCIATION: Stressed syllables Listen and repeat again. Which nationality words are stressed on the last syllable? 🎧12

Country	Nationality
China	Chinese
Japan	Japanese
Portugal	Portuguese
Australia	Australian
Brazil	Brazilian
Peru	Peruvian
Korea	Korean
Mexico	Mexican
the United States	American
Spain	Spanish
the United Kingdom	British
Turkey	Turkish

The same syllable is stressed		A different syllable is stressed	
Bra ZIL	Bra ZIL ian	CHI na	Chi NESE

C Where is each flag from? Write your answers. Tell a partner.

1. Canada
   It's the _____ flag.

2. Spain
   It's the _____ flag.

3. Jamaica
   It's the _____ flag.

4. China
   It's the _____ flag.

D Where are you from? What language(s) do you speak? Tell a partner.

LISTENING

A *Where in the World?* is a TV game show. Listen to each clue. Then circle the correct answer. 🎧13

1. a. the United States
   b. Canada
   c. Mexico
2. a. Canada
   b. Brazil
   c. the United Kingdom
3. a. Australia
   b. Argentina
   c. New Zealand
4. a. France
   b. the United States
   c. China
5. a. Brazil
   b. Chile
   c. Peru
6. a. Thailand
   b. Vietnam
   c. Malaysia

WORD BANK
city
country

B **Listen for confirmation.** Listen. Check your answers in **A**. 🎧14

> ✓ That's right. / That's correct.
> ✗ That's wrong. / That's incorrect.

C People from New Zealand are New Zealanders. They are also called "Kiwis." Look at your answers in **A**. Name each nationality.

Machu Picchu, Peru

SPEAKING

A Listen to the conversation. Where is Ana from? Where is Haru from? 🎧15

Haru: Excuse me. Are you in this class?

Ana: Yes, I am. Are you?

Haru: Yeah. Hi, my name's <u>Haru</u>.

Ana: Hi, I'm <u>Ana</u>.

Haru: Great to meet you.

Ana: You, too. So, where are you from, <u>Haru</u>?

Haru: <u>Japan</u>.

Ana: Cool. Which city?

Haru: <u>Tokyo</u>. How about you? Where are you from?

Ana: <u>Bogota, Colombia</u>.

Tokyo, Japan

B Now practice the conversation in **A** with a partner. Replace the underlined words with your own information.

C Think of a famous person. Write his or her information below.

Name: _____

City and country: _____

D Imagine you are a famous person at a party. Meet three people using the Speaking Strategy.

  “ Hi, I'm Rafael Nadal.

      Hi, Rafael. Where are you from? ”

  “ I'm from Spain.

      Really? Which city? ”

SPEAKING STRATEGY 🎧16
Asking where someone is from

Where are you from?
  (I'm from) Japan.
Really? Which city?
  (I'm from) Tokyo.
Really? Where exactly?
  (I'm from) a small town near Tokyo.
Are you from Colombia?
  Yes, I am. / No, I'm from Peru.

GRAMMAR

A Read the Unit 2, Lesson A Grammar Reference in the appendix. Complete the exercises. Then do the exercises below.

QUESTIONS WITH *WHO*			ANSWERS
Who	is 's	with you?	Tomas (is).

QUESTIONS WITH *WHERE*			ANSWERS
Where	are	you / they?	(I'm / We're / They're) **at** the beach / a museum.
Where	is 's	Nor?	(She's) **in** London / **at** her hotel.
		Machu Picchu?	(It's) **in** Peru.

B Nor is talking to Sara on the phone. Complete the conversation with *who*, *where*, *at*, or *in*. Then practice with a partner.

Sara: Hello?

Nor: <u>Sara</u>? Hi, it's <u>Nor</u>.

Sara: Hi, <u>Nor</u>! (1.) _____ are you?

Nor: I'm (2.) _____ <u>the UK</u>. Right now, I'm (3.) _____ <u>London</u>.

Sara: (4.) _____ exactly?

Nor: I'm (5.) _____ <u>Buckingham Palace</u>. Oh, and I'm here with a friend.

Sara: Really? (6.) _____'s with you?

Nor: <u>Irina</u>, from our English class. She lives (7.) _____ <u>London</u> now.

Sara: That's great! Say "hi" for me.

C Make a new conversation with a partner. Replace the underlined parts in **B** with the ideas below.

1. Use your own names and choose one of these two places.
   - Beijing, China / a cafe
   - Punta Cana, the Dominican Republic / a beach
2. At the end, use a classmate's name.

D Repeat Exercise **C**. Use a new city and place. Sit back-to-back with your partner and have the conversation. Try not to read the conversation.

E Work with a new partner. Talk about your "phone call" in Exercise **D**. Where is your partner? Who is your partner with?

“ Marta is in New York City with Diego. They're in Times Square.

**Punta Cana,
the Dominican Republic**

ACTIVE ENGLISH Try it out!

A **Directions:** Play in pairs.

1. Put a marker on *Start Here*.

2. Take turns. Flip a coin.

   Heads: Move one square. Tails: Move two squares.

3. Answer the question. For *Free Question!*, your partner asks you about a city or country. Write your answers.

4. The game ends when you both reach square 24. Check your answers. Each correct answer = 1 point. The person with the most points wins.

Heads

Tails

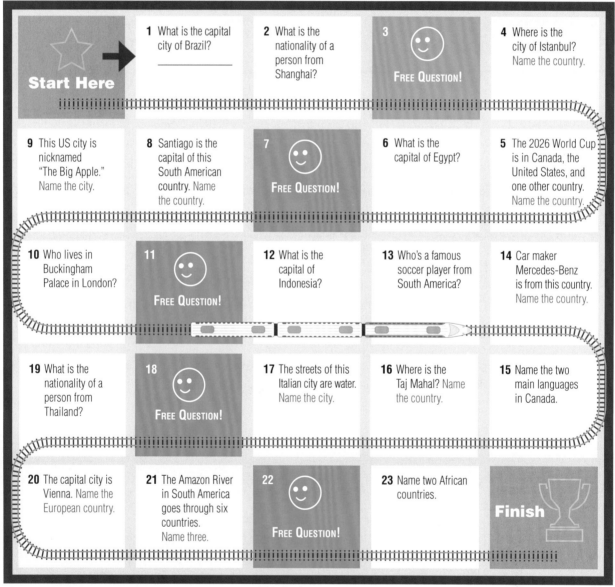

Start Here →

1 What is the capital city of Brazil? _____

2 What is the nationality of a person from Shanghai?

3 ☺ FREE QUESTION!

4 Where is the city of Istanbul? Name the country.

9 This US city is nicknamed "The Big Apple." Name the city.

8 Santiago is the capital of this South American country. Name the country.

7 ☺ FREE QUESTION!

6 What is the capital of Egypt?

5 The 2026 World Cup is in Canada, the United States, and one other country. Name the country.

10 Who lives in Buckingham Palace in London?

11 ☺ FREE QUESTION!

12 What is the capital of Indonesia?

13 Who's a famous soccer player from South America?

14 Car maker Mercedes-Benz is from this country. Name the country.

19 What is the nationality of a person from Thailand?

18 ☺ FREE QUESTION!

17 The streets of this Italian city are water. Name the city.

16 Where is the Taj Mahal? Name the country.

15 Name the two main languages in Canada.

20 The capital city is Vienna. Name the European country.

21 The Amazon River in South America goes through six countries. Name three.

22 ☺ FREE QUESTION!

23 Name two African countries.

Finish

Answers are on page 217.

2A GOALS Now I can . . .

Name countries and nationalities _____

Ask where someone is from _____

1. Yes, I can.
2. Mostly, yes.
3. Not yet.

VOCABULARY

A Look at the photo and read about the city of Rio. Is your city the same as Rio? Work with a partner.

1. Choose two words in **blue**.
2. Take turns asking your partner questions.

> " Rio is an old city.
> Is your city old?
> Yes, it is. "

FUN FACTS ABOUT RIO DE JANEIRO, BRAZIL

Rio is a **large** and **old** city.

Its nickname is "the Marvelous City" because the beaches are **beautiful**, the nightlife is **exciting**, and the people are **friendly**.

Rio is **famous** for . . .

- Carnival: Every year the streets are **crowded** and **busy** with people from all over Brazil and the world.
- Copacabana: This is a **relaxing** beach. It's also a **popular** place to play soccer.
- Sugar Loaf: This is a **big** mountain. It is 396 meters (1,299 feet) **tall**. From here, there's a **wonderful** view of the city.

Rio is an **interesting** city and a **fun** place to visit!

B Answer the questions with a partner.

1. Is your city big or small?
2. Is it interesting?
3. Are the people friendly?
4. Are the streets crowded? If yes, where and when?
5. What is your city famous for?
6. What is your favorite place in your city? Why?

WORD BANK
Opposites
big, large ⟷ small
old ⟷ new
interesting ⟷ boring

View of Rio de Janeiro from Sugar Loaf Mountain

A GREAT PLACE TO VISIT

Table Mountain

soccer stadium

Hi Cary,

Greetings! It's day six of my vacation. I'm in a big city of 4.7 million people. It's very exciting.

Right now I'm in a busy cafe on Long Street. There are a lot of restaurants and shops on Long Street. The streets are very crowded!

There are many interesting things to see and do here. Boulders Beach is beautiful. It's famous for penguins. They're really cute!

Penguins at Boulders Beach

There's also Table Mountain. It's a popular place. The view from there is really wonderful.

There are many soccer stadiums here. Do you like soccer? I don't!

I'm having a great time! Please say "hi" to everyone in Sydney for me!

Melissa

Some people call this city the *Mother City*.

A In one minute, write down any famous cities and places in your country on a piece of paper. Compare your list with a partner's. Why are the places famous?

B Read the email. Where is Melissa? In which city and country? Follow the steps below to guess.

1. Circle key words.

2. Write your guess:
   _____

3. Compare your answer with a partner's.

4. Check your answer at the bottom of the next page.

C **Read for details.** Read Melissa's note again. Circle **T** for *true* or **F** for *false*. Correct the false sentences to make them true.

1. Melissa is in Sydney.	**T F**
_____	
2. She's on vacation.	**T F**
_____	
3. She's in a big city.	**T F**
_____	
4. Long Street is not busy.	**T F**
_____	
5. Penguins are on Table Mountain.	**T F**
_____	
6. Melissa loves soccer.	**T F**
_____	
7. Her vacation is fun.	**T F**
_____	

D What place in this city do you want to visit?

Khaju Bridge, Isfahan, Iran

LISTENING

A Look at the photo. Work with a partner. What words describe this place?

B Listen to John talk about the city of Isfahan. What country is it in? Write your answer. 🎧18

_____

C **Listen for details.** Listen. Match the places (1–5) to the words on the right (a–h). Some places have more than one answer. 🎧19

1. Iran _____
2. the Iranian people _____
3. Khaju Bridge _____
4. the main square _____
5. Isfahan _____

a. beautiful
b. big
c. famous
d. friendly

e. wonderful
f. old
g. relaxing
h. interesting

D Do you want to visit Isfahan? Why or why not? Tell a partner.

Exercise B, page 25 answer:
Cape Town, South Africa

GRAMMAR

A Read the Unit 2, Lesson B Grammar Reference in the appendix. Complete the exercises. Then do the exercises below.

ADJECTIVES WITH *BE*							
	be	Adjective			*be*		Adjective	Noun
Copacabana	**is**	relaxing.	It	**is**	a	popular	place.
The penguins	**are**	cute.	There	**are**		big	stadiums.

B Take turns describing your city with a partner. Use adjectives with *be*.

C Look at the sentences in the grammar chart above. Work with a partner. Rewrite each one as a question.

Copacabana is beautiful. → *Is Copacabana beautiful?*

D Read the sentences. In your notebook, rewrite each one as a question.

1. The food is good.
2. It's a fun place.
3. The streets are crowded.
4. The nightlife is exciting.
5. The people are friendly.
6. It's famous for music.

E Think of a place. Take turns guessing your partner's place. Ask questions like the ones in **D**.

66 Are the streets crowded?

No, they aren't. 99

66 Is it a relaxing place?

Yes, it is. 99

This popular tea house in Isfahan has interesting decorations.

In the botanical garden in Montreal, Canada, there are interesting plants and beautiful buildings.

ACTIVE ENGLISH Try it out!

A Look at the photo. Is this a good place to visit on vacation?

B Where is a good place for vacation? Write your ideas in the chart under Place 1 or in your notebook.

	Place 1 (my idea)	Place 2	Place 3	Place 4
Place				
Where is it?				
How is it there?				

C Interview three classmates. Write their ideas in the chart under Places 2, 3, and 4.

D Choose one place for a vacation. Explain your choice to a partner.

E **WRITING** In your notebook, write about your choice. Use the information from the chart in **B**.

> My choice is Montreal, Canada. It's an old and beautiful city. French is the main language in Montreal. Montreal is busy with students from around the world. The area is famous for maple syrup. The French food is good there, too!

F Exchange papers with a partner. What's your partner's choice? Is it an interesting place?

2B GOALS   Now I can . . .

Talk about a city _____

Describe a good vacation place _____

1. Yes, I can.
2. Mostly, yes.
3. Not yet.

GLOBAL VOICES

A Use your dictionary. Look up the words in the box. Then complete the sentences. Tell your partner.

1. I'm from _____.
2. My father's family is from _____.
3. My mother's family is from _____.

WORD BANK
family
father
mother

B Watch the video about Andrés Ruzo. Circle the country names that you hear.

Australia _____   Nicaragua _____

China _____   Peru _____

Colombia _____   Spain _____

Iceland _____   United States _____

C Write the nationality next to the country name in **B**. (*Iceland → Icelandic*). Then complete the sentence.

Andrés Ruzo is _____, Nicaraguan, and _____.

D Watch the video. Match the words and make sentences.

1. Lima is   a. old.
2. Cusco is   b. many Spanish speakers.
3. Chinandega is famous for   c. big.
4. Miami has   d. volcanoes.
                                     e. busy.
                                     f. farming.

WORD BANK
farming
volcano

E Now make sentences about your city. Tell a partner.

1. My city is _____ and _____.
2. It's famous for _____.

Andrés Ruzo looking at the San Cristóbal volcano in Chinandega, Nicaragua

3

POSSESSIONS

LOOK AT THE PHOTO. ANSWER THE QUESTIONS.

1. What is the man's favorite thing?
2. Is it old or new?

WARM-UP VIDEO

A Watch the first 10 seconds of the video. Complete the question.

What do you _____ with you?

B Answer the question in **A**. (Use your dictionary to help you.) Tell a partner one thing.

C Read the list. Look up any words you don't know in your dictionary.

☐ a book

☐ a camera

☐ a phone

☐ a soccer ball

☐ a wallet

☐ keys

D Watch the first minute of the video. Check (✓) the things in **C** you see.

E Watch the video. What do people carry? Name one more thing.

F Look at the list in **C**. What do you carry? Circle your answers. Tell a partner.

A man sits in front of his car in Trinidad, Cuba.

GOALS

Lesson A
/ Identify everyday objects
/ Give and reply to thanks

Lesson B
/ Describe objects that are important to you
/ Talk about things that are near and not near

VOCABULARY

A Look at the photo and caption below. Answer the question with a partner.

B Read the words. Then listen and repeat. 🎧20

1. a **backpack**
2. a **gift card**
3. **headphones**
4. **movie tickets**
5. a **laptop**
6. **sunglasses**
7. a **wallet**
8. a **watch**

C Match four of the words in **B** with the items on the right.

D Look at the gifts in **B**. Choose one. Ask your partner questions about their gift.

" What's this?
    It's a watch. "

" Is it your favorite?
    No, it isn't. "

E Answer the questions with a partner.

1. What items in **B** do you have?
2. What is the best gift for a student?

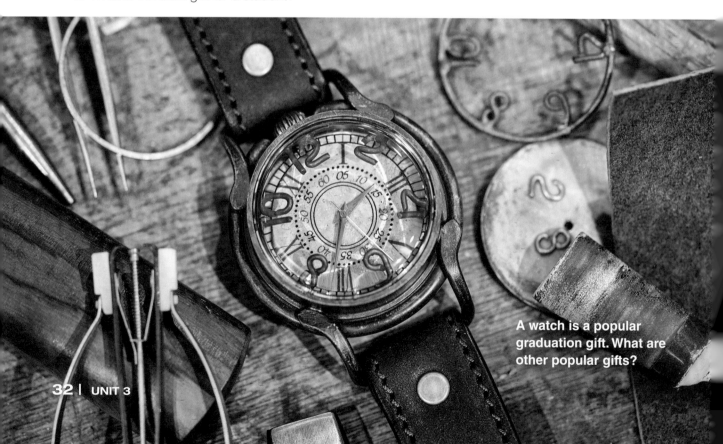

A watch is a popular graduation gift. What are other popular gifts?

Liu Xuchang celebrates his birthday with his family in Shanghai, China.

LISTENING

A Tak is buying a gift for Sue. Listen and circle the correct answers. 🎧21

1. Sue is Tak's **classmate** / **friend**.
2. Tak is buying her a **graduation** / **birthday** gift.
3. Sue likes **baseball** / **soccer**.
4. She likes **hip-hop** / **pop** music.

B Listen. Number the three items (1, 2, 3) as you hear them. (You will not number all of the items.) 🎧22

sunglasses _____   a gift card _____   a watch _____

headphones _____   movie tickets _____   a backpack _____

C **Listen for details.** Follow the steps. 🎧22

1. Write items 1, 2, and 3 from **B** in the chart below.
2. Listen again. What do Tak and Martina say about each gift? Circle your answers.

1.	**boring** / **fun** / **popular**
2.	**beautiful** / **expensive** / **nice**
3.	**not expensive** / **not boring** / **favorite**

D Look at the words in **B**. What do you think? What is a good second choice for Sue's gift?

SPEAKING

A Listen to the conversation. Then practice it with two partners. 🎧23

Sun: Oh, no . . .

Paula: What's wrong, Sun?

Sun: My wallet. Where's my <u>wallet</u>?

Paula: Is it in your pocket?

Sun: Um . . . no.

Paula: Is it in your backpack?

Sun: No, it's not. I can't find it anywhere!

Man: Hmm . . . what's this? Excuse me, miss?

Sun: Yes?

Man: Is this your <u>wallet</u>?

Sun: Yes, it is! Thank you very much!

Man: You're welcome.

Common lost items: 1. TV remote, 2. phone, 3. keys, 4. glasses, 5. wallet / purse

B Practice the conversation again. Take a different role. Replace the underlined word in **A** to ask about the items below.

key

credit card

charger

C Imagine you lost one of these important items. Create a short conversation. Use the Speaking Strategy to thank and reply to each other formally.

movie tickets

notebook

phone

sunglasses

SPEAKING STRATEGY 🎧24

Giving and Replying to Thanks

Saying *Thank you*		Replies
Thank you very much.	**formal**	You're welcome.
Thank you.	↑	My pleasure.
Thanks a lot.	↓	Sure, no problem.
Thanks.	**informal**	You bet.

D Choose a different item in **C**. Repeat your conversation. This time, thank and reply to each other informally.

GRAMMAR

A Read the Unit 3, Lesson A Grammar Reference in the appendix. Complete the exercises. Then do the exercises below.

SPELLING RULES FOR FORMING PLURAL NOUNS		
Most plural nouns are formed by adding *s*:	camera ➔ camera**s**	pen ➔ pen**s**
For nouns ending in a <u>vowel</u> + *y*, add *s*:	bo**y** ➔ bo**ys**	
For nouns ending in a <u>consonant</u> + *y*, drop the *y* and add *ies*:	dictionar**y** ➔ dictionar**ies**	
For nouns ending in a <u>vowel</u> + *o*, add *s*:	radi**o** ➔ radi**os**	
For nouns ending in a <u>consonant</u> + *o*, add *s* with some nouns and *es* with others:	phot**o** ➔ phot**os**	potat**o** ➔ potat**oes**
For nouns ending in *ch*, *sh*, *ss*, or *x*, add *es*:	clas**s** ➔ clas**ses**	
For nouns ending in *f* / *fe*, change it to *ve* + *s*:	kni**fe** ➔ kni**ves**	lea**f** ➔ lea**ves**

> **Singular and Plural Count Nouns**
> It's <u>an</u> ID card.
> I'm <u>a</u> student.
> We're students.

B **PRONUNCIATION: Plural endings** Listen and repeat. Then practice saying the singular and plural forms of the nouns. 🎧25

class ➔ classes	dish ➔ dishes
watch ➔ watches	bus ➔ buses
backpack ➔ backpacks	laptop ➔ laptops
notebook ➔ notebooks	wallet ➔ wallets
camera ➔ cameras	ID card ➔ ID cards
key ➔ keys	umbrella ➔ umbrellas

> There are three different ways to pronounce plural endings.

C Read the rules of the guessing game. Then play the game with a partner.

1. Write the number *1* on five pieces of paper.
2. Write the number *2* on five pieces of paper.
3. Mix up the pieces of paper and place them face down.
4. Choose a word from the list in **B** and pick up a piece of paper.
5. If your paper says 1, draw one item (for example, *a watch* or *an umbrella*).
6. If your paper says 2, draw two items (for example, *two keys*).
7. Your partner guesses the answer and then spells out the word.

> " I think the answer is "a camera." That's C-A-M-E-R-A.
>
> You're right! "

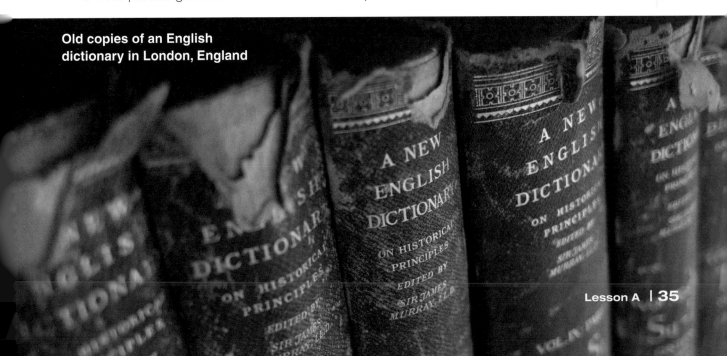

Old copies of an English dictionary in London, England

ACTIVE ENGLISH Try it out!

A Jane is giving Lucas a gift. Practice the conversation with a partner.

Lucas: What's this . . . a watch? Wow, it's cool. Thanks, Jane.
I really like it.

Jane: I'm glad you like it, Lucas.

B Practice the conversation again with a different gift idea. Use the language in the box to talk about the gift.

When people say *Thank you* for a gift, they also say . . .		
Thanks.	I really like it / them.	
	I like it / them a lot.	
	It's	cool / beautiful / great / nice / perfect.
	They're	

C Think of a gift. Write the name of the gift on a small piece of paper. Fold the paper.

a watch   sunglasses

D Work with a partner. Follow these gift-giving steps.

1. Exchange your papers.
2. Thank your partner for the gift. Say something about it.
3. Write the name of the gift in the box.
4. Do this four more times with new partners.

Gifts
1. _____
2. _____
3. _____
4. _____
5. _____

E Tell a new partner about your gifts. Which is your favorite?

66 My gifts are a watch, sunglasses, movie tickets . . .

66 The sunglasses!   What's your favorite gift? 99

3A GOALS Now I can . . .

Identify everyday objects _____

Give and reply to thanks _____

1. Yes, I can.
2. Mostly, yes.
3. Not yet.

VOCABULARY

A Look at the photo and read the caption. Answer the question with a partner.

B Read the sentences. Look up any words you don't know. Then, write the words in blue from the sentences in the Word Bank.

1. My room **is** / **isn't** clean.
2. _____ is the most **expensive** thing in my room.
3. _____ is the most **important** thing in my room.
4. It **is** / **isn't** easy to find things in my room.
5. I **feel** / **don't feel** good about my room.

WORD BANK
Opposites

_____ ⟷ messy
_____ ⟷ hard
_____ ⟷ cheap
_____ ⟷ bad
_____ ⟷ unimportant

C Complete the sentences in **B**.

D Tell a partner about your room.

" My room is clean.
Is your room clean?

No, it's not.
It's messy. "

Is this room the same
as, or different from,
your room?

READING

WHO IS **MARIE KONDO?**

Marie Kondo

Is your room messy? Many people's rooms are not tidy[1]. Their rooms are filled with clothes, books, papers, and more. They feel bad about their rooms. They need help.

Marie Kondo helps them. She's an expert[2]. She's good at organizing[3].

Marie is on TV. Her show is *Tidying up with Marie Kondo*. It's a fun show. She's also a writer. Her book is very popular. It's in more than 30 countries. It's in Chinese, Spanish, Korean, French, and many other languages. She's famous.

Here are some good tips from Marie Kondo:

- In your room, there are different groups of things (clothes, books, papers). To tidy up, start with the clothes first and then the books and the papers. This order is important.
- Look at your clothes. Don't keep[4] everything. This is hard.
- It's the same with your books and papers. Throw away the extra things.
- Do some things make you happy? Keep those things.

These are some of the tips from Marie Kondo. There are many more on her TV show and in her book! 🎧26

[1] A **tidy** room is not messy.
[2] Marie Kondo is an **expert** in tidying. She knows a lot about it.
[3] When you **organize**, you take a messy room and make it tidy.
[4] Don't **keep** everything. Give some things to another person.

A Look at the photos. Then circle the correct answers.

1. The clothes in the drawer are **messy** / **tidy**.

2. Marie Kondo helps people. She's **good** / **bad** at organizing.

B **Scan for information.** Read the first two paragraphs. Check your answers in **A**.

C Read the article about Marie Kondo. What exactly does the article say? Make sentences with columns A–D. (Only two of the sentences use column C.)

A	B	C	D
Marie Kondo Her book People's rooms The tips Her show	are is	a an	expert. messy. fun. famous. good. popular. writer.

Mary Kondo helps people to be more tidy.

D Work with a partner. Follow the steps.

1. Look at the information in **C**. Don't look at the article.

2. What is the article about? Take turns. Say one fact from the article.

Student A: Marie Kondo is an expert.

Student B: She's famous.

Student A: She helps people.

Student B: Her book . . .

E Read the tips. Correct the errors.

1. There are groups of things, like clothes, books, and dishes.

2. Start with the books.

3. Keep everything.

F Are Marie Kondo's tips good? Talk about them with a partner.

LISTENING

A **Listen for the main idea.** Read the sentence. Then listen. Circle your answer. 🎧27

Anna is throwing away her old **books / clothes / photos** today.

WORD BANK
keep ⟷ throw away

B Listen. Write the answers for ❶ (*Where is Anna?*) only. 🎧28

	❶ Where is Anna?	❷ Who is she with?
Photo #1		
Photo #2		
Photo #3		

WORD BANK
parents

C Listen again. Now write answers for ❷ (*Who is she with?*). 🎧28

D Listen one more time. Circle **T** for *true* or **F** for *false*. 🎧28

1. Anna is 20 years old now.   **T**   **F**
2. In photo #1, she's in front of her school.   **T**   **F**
3. She's on vacation in photo #2.   **T**   **F**
4. She's at her school in photo #3.   **T**   **F**

E Complete the sentence. Tell a partner.

I **keep / throw away** old photos.

Tower Bridge, London

GRAMMAR

A Read the Unit 3, Lesson B Grammar Reference in the appendix. Complete the exercises. Then do the exercises below.

	THIS / THAT / THESE / THOSE	
	Near	**Not Near**
Singular	❶ **This is** my ID card. ❶ A: Bill, **this is** my friend Nadia. B: Hi, Nadia. Nice to meet you.	❷ A: Who**'s that** over there? B: **That's** Marie Kondo. ❷ **That's** an expensive watch!
Plural	❸ **These** headphones **are** really good. ❸ A: **These are** my parents. B: It's nice to meet you, Mr. and Mrs. Kim.	❹ A: **Are those** your photos? B: Yes, they are.

❶ Use *this* to talk about a person or a thing near to you. Use *this is* on the phone or to introduce a person.
❷ Use *that* to talk about a person or a thing that is not near to you.
❸ Use *these* to talk about two or more people or things near to you. Use *these* to introduce two or more people.
❹ Use *those* to talk about two or more people or things that are not near to you.

B Play this game in groups of four.

1. Choose a column in the chart. Write your name.

2. Student 1 flips two coins. Make a sentence.

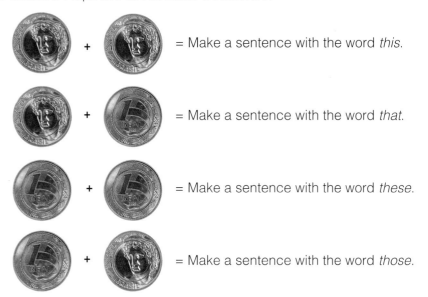

= Make a sentence with the word *this*.

= Make a sentence with the word *that*.

= Make a sentence with the word *these*.

= Make a sentence with the word *those*.

3. If the sentence is correct, put a check (✓) next to your word. If it is incorrect, do nothing.

4. Repeat these steps for Students 2, 3, and 4. Do not repeat another student's sentence.

5. At the end of the game, count check marks. The player with the most check marks wins!

Name:	Name:	Name:	Name:
this	this	this	this
that	that	that	that
these	these	these	these
those	those	those	those

ACTIVE ENGLISH Try it out!

A Think of an old object in your room. Draw a picture of it. Then complete the information.

The object: _____

1. Is it your favorite?	☐ yes	☐ no
2. Is it expensive?	☐ yes	☐ no
3. Is it important to you?	☐ yes	☐ no
4. Is it easy to buy?	☐ yes	☐ no

B **WRITING** Use your notes in **A**. Write about the object.

> This shirt is old and cheap. It isn't my favorite, but it's important. It's from my soccer club. It isn't easy to buy.

ℹ Using *but*

Use *but* to join two opposite ideas.
*This shirt isn't my favorite, **but** it's important.*
*That room is crowded **but** clean.*

C Show your picture in **A** to five classmates. Tell them about your object.

1. Ask for their advice: keep it, throw it away, or give it away?
2. Write their answers in the chart.

	Classmate	Choice	Reason
Example	Lucy	☐ keep it ☑ throw it away ☐ give it away	It's old.
1		☐ keep it ☐ throw it away ☐ give it away	
2		☐ keep it ☐ throw it away ☐ give it away	
3		☐ keep it ☐ throw it away ☐ give it away	
4		☐ keep it ☐ throw it away ☐ give it away	
5		☐ keep it ☐ throw it away ☐ give it away	

D Tell a partner about the advice and your choice.

❝ There are three votes for "keep it." My choice is to keep the shirt.

3B GOALS Now I can . . .

Describe objects that are important to me _____

Talk about things that are near and not near _____

1. Yes, I can.
2. Mostly, yes.
3. Not yet.

GLOBAL VOICES

A Look up the word *gadget* in your dictionary. What is one gadget you use? Write your answer. Share it with a partner.

_____

B Watch the first part of the video. What gadgets do you see? Write their names.

1. _____

2. _____

3. _____

4. *coffee machine* _____

5. _____

6. _____

C Watch Ashley and Clare talk about their favorite gadgets. Circle your answers.

Ashley

1. I'm **very** / **not very** busy.

2. This phone has a **good** / **great** camera.

3. The photos are really **good** / **great**.

4. My phone is really **expensive** / **important**.

Clare

5. Clare's coffee machine is **clean** / **new**.

6. It's **cheap** / **expensive**.

7. It makes coffee in **one minute** / **two minutes**.

8. It has **five** / **ten** different kinds of coffee.

D Draw or show a picture of your favorite gadget. Tell a partner about it. Use at least three of the words in the box.

cheap	expensive	fun	good	new	popular

" This is my favorite gadget. It's a drone with a really good camera. It's a lot of fun!

REAL WORLD LINK BIG CITY OR SMALL TOWN?

A busy street in Bangkok, Thailand

A Look at the photos. Complete the sentences with the words in the box. Use each word once.

~~big~~ busy capital friendly market nightlife small

1. **Bangkok** is the _____ of Thailand. It's a _____*big*_____ city of over eight million (8,000,000) people.

2. The streets are _____ with people and cars.

3. It's famous for its shopping, food, and exciting _____.

4. **Tha Kha** is a _____ district with 5,500 people. It's one hour from Bangkok.

5. It's a relaxing place with _____ people.

6. It's famous for its floating _____.

B Unscramble the words to make questions about the two places.

Bangkok

1. Bangkok / is / where   _____*Where is Bangkok*_____?
2. is / Bangkok / large / a / city   _____?
3. streets / crowded / are / the   _____?
4. Bangkok / place / boring / a / is _____?

Tha Kha

5. is / Tha Kha / where   _____?
6. is / city / it / big / a   _____?
7. people / the / friendly / are   _____ there?
8. it / famous for / its nightlife / is _____?

C Work with a partner. Ask and answer the questions in B.

Student A: Ask about Bangkok.

Student B: Ask about Tha Kha.

A market in Tha Kha

D Which place—Bangkok or Tha Kha—is more interesting to you? Why? Tell a partner.

> Bangkok is an exciting place, but I'm not into big, busy cities.

E With a partner, think of a big city and a small town in your country. Write them in the chart.

Big city:	Small town:
It's in	It's in
It's famous for	It's famous for
Life is _____ there.	Life is _____ there.
The people are	The people are

F With the same partner, complete the four sentences in **E** to describe each place: Where is it? Why is it famous? How is life there? How are the people? Use the words below.

beautiful	cheap	expensive	good	popular
big / large	clean	famous	interesting	relaxing
boring	crowded	friendly	new	small
busy	exciting	fun	old	other: _____

G **You Choose** Choose an option to present your two places. Use photos and your sentences from **E**.

Option 1: Make a video about the two places.

Option 2: Make a poster about the two places.

Option 3: Write a social media post about the two places.

H Work with another pair. Take turns. Thank the speakers for their presentation.

Pair 1: Present your two places.

Pair 2: Say your opinion: Is Pair 1's city or town more interesting to you? Why?

> Our two places are Osaka and the small city of Takayama . . .
>
> My choice is Takayama. Osaka is fun, but it's expensive and crowded. Also, . . .

45

People in Bangladesh traveling by ferry after vacation

GOALS

Lesson A
/ Explain what you're doing
/ Greet people and ask how they are

Lesson B
/ Talk about classes and school subjects
/ Talk about things you're learning these days

ACTIVITIES

LOOK AT THE PHOTO. ANSWER THE QUESTIONS.

1. Where are the people?
2. What are they doing?

WARM-UP VIDEO

A Look at the activities in the box. Watch your teacher act out the meaning of each word.

drinking	exercising	talking
eating	studying	teaching

B Read the question. Then watch the video with the sound off. As you watch, use the words in **A** to tell a partner.

What are Leah and her friends doing?

She is _____.

He is _____.

They are _____.

C Watch again with the sound on. Complete the sentences with a word in **A**.

1. Leah is _____ business.
2. Sophia is _____ history.
3. Emile is _____ at the gym.
4. Renee is _____ lunch and _____ on the phone.
5. The professor is _____ a class.
6. Paolo and Leah are _____ for a test. They're also _____ coffee.

D Cover your answers in **A–C**. Watch again with the sound off. What are they doing? As you watch, tell a partner.

VOCABULARY

A Say the words in blue with your teacher. Do you know any of these words?

1. She's **studying** for a test.
2. She's **watching** TV.
3. He's **texting** a friend.
4. She's **exercising** and **listening** to music.
5. He's **talking** on the phone.
6. He's **eating** pizza and **drinking** soda.
7. They're **going** to school.
8. She's **shopping**.

> **ℹ Notice**
> go <u>to</u> school
> listen <u>to</u> music
> study <u>for</u> a test
> talk <u>on</u> the phone

B What are these people doing? Match each sentence in **A** with a photo.

C Cover the sentences in **A**. Point to a person and ask a partner a question.

> “ What's she doing?
> She's studying. ”

LISTENING

A Say the words in the Word Bank with your teacher. Look up new words in your dictionary.

WORD BANK
do homework
run
wait for (a person, a bus)

B Listen to three conversations. What is happening in each? 🎧29 Write important words, not sentences.

Conversation 1: _____

Conversation 2: _____

Conversation 3: _____

C **Listen for specific information.** Listen again. Circle the correct answer(s). One item has two correct answers. 🎧29

1. The phone is _____.
   a. a gift   b. popular   c. expensive
2. Gabby and Jim talk _____.
   a. now   b. later   c. tomorrow
3. Ben says the video is _____.
   a. exciting   b. relaxing   c. interesting

D Listen to the conversations one more time. Also listen to the three answers. Circle A, B, or C. 🎧30

1. What is the man doing?   A   B   C
2. What is Gabby doing?   A   B   C
3. What is Ben doing?   A   B   C

E Check your answers in **D**. Do they match your notes in **B**? Tell a partner.

A woman running in a park in Utah, US

People wait for the
subway in Paris, France.

SPEAKING

A Listen to the conversation. Then answer the questions with a partner. 🎧31

Monique: Hello?

Luis: Hey, Monique. It's Luis.

Monique: Hi, Luis. How are you doing?

Luis: Fine. How about you?

Monique: So-so.

Luis: Yeah? What's wrong?

Monique: I'm waiting for the bus. It's late!

Luis: Sorry to hear that.

Monique: What are you doing, Luis?

Luis: Not much. I'm watching TV.

1. How is Luis? How is Monique?

2. What is Monique doing? What is Luis doing?

B PRONUNCIATION: Combining words with *how* Listen and repeat. 🎧32

How are you doing? → Sounds like *How're you doing?*

Fine. How about you? → Sounds like *How 'bout you?*

C Practice the conversation in **A** with a partner.

D Complete the conversations below. Use the Speaking Strategy to help you. Then practice the conversations with a partner.

1. **A:** Hi, _____. How _____?

   B: _____ -so.

   A: Yeah? _____?

   B: I'm studying for a test. It's hard!

2. **A:** Hi, _____. How _____?

   B: Pretty _____. How _____?

   A: All _____. What _____?

   B: Not much. I'm watching a video.

SPEAKING STRATEGY 🎧33
Greeting People and Asking How They Are
☺ **A:** Hi, . . . How are you doing?   **B:** Fine. / OK. / All right. / Pretty good. How about you?   **A:** I'm fine.
☹ **A:** Hi, . . . How are you doing?   **B:** So-so.   **A:** Yeah? What's wrong?   **B:** I'm waiting for the bus. It's late!

E Greet four classmates and ask how they are.

GRAMMAR

A Read the Unit 4, Lesson A Grammar Reference in the appendix. Complete the exercises. Then do the exercises below.

THE PRESENT CONTINUOUS: AFFIRMATIVE AND NEGATIVE STATEMENTS		
I'm / You're / He's / She's / We're / They're	(not) **watching**	TV.

YES / NO AND WH- QUESTIONS				
Question Word	*be*		verb + *-ing*	Short Answers
	Are	you		Yes, I am. / No, I'm not.
	Is	he	**studying?**	Yes, he is. / No, he's not.
	Are	they		Yes, they are. / No, they're not.
What	are	you	**doing?**	(I'm) **watching** TV.
	is	he		(He's) **watching** TV.
Who	are	you	**texting?**	(I'm texting) my friend.
	is	he		(He's texting) his friend.

B Work with a partner.
Student A: Turn to page 212. Read the directions.

Student B: Look at the photo. What are Omar and Alba doing? Write sentences.

C Your partner's photo is similar to yours, but there are some differences. Find the differences together. Ask questions.

❝ In your photo, is Alba texting?

No, she's not. She's . . . ❞

D Repeat **B** and **C** with this new photo.

ACTIVE ENGLISH Try it out!

A Follow the steps below to play this game.

1. Get into a group of three. Read the actions. Look up new words.

dancing to rap music	saying *hi* to a friend on the street
drinking hot coffee	shopping for a gift
exercising and listening to music	studying for an exam
playing a video game	texting someone
playing soccer	waiting for a bus
reading a funny book	watching a sad movie

2. Write each action on a piece of paper. Mix the papers and put them face down. Then cover the actions in the box.

3. **Student A:** Take a paper and act out the action. You cannot talk! You have one minute.

   Students B and C: What is Student A doing? Guess by asking *Yes / No* questions. For each correct answer, the group gets a point.

   " Are you playing soccer?

4. Take turns as the actor and repeat step 3 until you use all the papers. Which group has the most points?

B Play the game again. This time, use your own ideas.

4A GOALS   Now I can . . .

Explain what I'm doing _____

Greet people and ask how they are _____

1. Yes, I can.
2. Mostly, yes.
3. Not yet.

VOCABULARY

A The words in blue are subjects people study in school. Say them with your teacher. Then add ideas to the list.

- art
- business
- engineering
- graphic design
- history
- hospitality
- information technology (IT)
- law
- math
- nursing
- science

My idea: _____

B Read about the people. Pay attention to the words in blue. Match a person with a reason (a–d).

Yousef: I'm going to college in Canada. I'm majoring in business.

Pedro: I'm studying hospitality. It's a two-year program.

Emma: I'm taking an art class.

Li-Na: I'm preparing for the university entrance exam.

a. I'm planning to work in a large hotel in the future.

b. I'm doing it for fun.

c. I'm planning to go to college.

d. I'm planning to work for a Canadian company after graduation.

C What is each person in **B** doing and why?

Student A: Talk about Yousef and Pedro.

Student B: Talk about Emma and Li-Na.

66 Li-Na is preparing for . . .

She's planning to . . . 99

D Talk about yourself. Use two or more of the sentences.

I go to . . .

I'm majoring in . . .

I'm studying . . .

I'm taking a(n) . . . class.

I'm preparing for . . .

I'm planning to . . .

i *plan to + verb*

I'm **planning to** go to college.

These students are taking an art class.

POPULAR ONLINE CLASSES

Today, many famous universities are offering classes online[1] to everyone for free. What are some of the most popular classes and why?

Five Favorites

Classes in computer science and (1.) _____ are the most popular. Today, many people are studying these subjects. In the future, they are planning to work in tech because there are many jobs and the pay[2] is good.

Classes about (2.) _____ are also popular. Today, many people's lives are very busy, and this is hard. In these classes, people learn to feel good. A very popular class on this topic, *The Science of Well-Being*, is Yale University's most popular course ever.

Today, more people are studying or working in other countries. For this reason, many people are taking (3.) _____ classes. (English, Mandarin, Korean, and Spanish are the most popular.) Other people are preparing for an English-language (4.) _____ like the TOEFL or IELTS.

At Harvard University, there is a famous class called *Justice*. In it, a professor from the university's (5.) _____ school talks about different social problems. He asks the question: "What's the right thing to do?" The class is interesting, and many people take it for fun.

Learn more

Peking University (in China), Stanford University (in the US), UNAM (in Mexico), Yonsei University (in South Korea), and many others offer free classes on the internet. To learn more, do a search for a college's name and "free online classes." 🎧34

[1]*When something is **online** it's on the internet.*
[2]***Pay** is money for work.*

Professor Michael Sandel teaches the *Justice* class at Harvard University. People can also watch the lectures online for free.

A Prepare to read the article.

- Look at the photo and read the caption.
- Read the title and the paragraph below it.
- For 1–3 below, circle **T** for *true* or **F** for *false*.

The reading is about popular college classes. These classes are _____.

1. free ($0)   **T   F**
2. for college students only   **T   F**
3. on the internet   **T   F**

B Look at the list below. In your opinion, which are popular online classes? Choose five ideas. Tell a partner.

art	IT
exam	law
foreign language	nursing
hospitality	well-being

C **Infer information.** Read the article. Write words from **B** in the reading.

D Look at your answers in 1–5 in the reading.

1. Why are people taking these classes? Underline the reasons in the article.

2. Explain your answers to a partner. Use your own words. Take turns.

E Answer the questions with a partner.

1. Are any classes in the article interesting to you?

2. Find out about one more free online class. What does it teach? Why is it interesting to you?

In Berlin, the capital of Germany, there are many murals painted by artists from around the world.

LISTENING

A Look at the photo. Do you know anything about Berlin? Tell a partner.

B Read the question and 1–3. Then listen. Write a word in each blank. 🎧35

These days, people from many countries are studying in Berlin.
Why is it a good place to study?

1. It's a world capital of _____ and _____.

2. The schools are good, but they aren't _____.

3. It's an _____ and interesting city.

C **Listen for specific information.** Read 1–4. Then listen and circle **T** for *true* or **F** for *false*. Change the false sentences so they are true. 🎧36

1. There are many tech companies in Berlin.   **T   F**

2. Some universities are almost free for foreign students.   **T   F**

3. At German universities, classes are in German only.   **T   F**

4. Berlin is famous for its history, classical music, and food.   **T   F**

D Work with a partner.

1. Read the question in **B** again. Cover your answers in **B** and **C** and explain.

2. Is Berlin interesting to you? Why or why not?

E With your partner, complete the sentence with the name of a city. Give two reasons.

In my country, _____ is a good place to study.

1. _____

2. _____

GRAMMAR

A Read the Unit 4, Lesson B Grammar Reference in the appendix. Complete the exercises. Then do the exercises below.

> ### THE PRESENT CONTINUOUS: EXTENDED TIME
> A: **Are** you **taking** any classes online <u>this term</u>?
> B: Yes, I**'m taking** an art history class online.
>
> A: What **are** you **doing** <u>these days</u>?
> B: I**'m preparing** for the university entrance exam.

B Two old friends meet on the street. Complete the conversation with the present continuous. Use the words given. Then practice with a partner.

Carlos: Hey, Igor!

Igor: Hi, Carlos!

Carlos: How are you doing?

Igor: I'm all right. How about you?

Carlos: Pretty good. So, (1.) _____ (what / you / do) these days?

Igor: (2.) _____ (I / study) at State University.

Carlos: Really? (3.) _____ (What / you / major) in?

Igor: Graphic design. What about you? (4.) _____ (you / work) or (5.) _____ (you / go) to school?

Carlos: Both. (6.) _____ (I / work) part-time at a cafe.
(7.) _____ (I / take) two classes at City College this term, too.

Igor: (8.) _____? (What / you / study)

Carlos: Photography and art history.

Igor: (9.) _____ (you / enjoy) the classes?

Carlos: Yeah. They're fun and (10.) _____ (I / learn) a lot.

C Make a new conversation. Use your own information in **B**.

Photographer Joel Sartore taking photos of penguins

ACTIVE ENGLISH Try it out!

A **WRITING** Answer the questions.

Studying English: Interview Questions

1. Why are you studying English?
   - ☐ I'm doing it for fun.
   - ☐ I'm planning to travel.
   - ☐ I'm majoring in English.
   - ☐ I'm doing it for my job.
   - ☐ I'm preparing for an exam.
   - ☐ Other: _____

2. What are you learning in your English class these days?

   _____

   _____

   _____

3. How are you doing in your English class? Is your English improving?

   _____

   _____

4. Outside of class, how are you practicing English?

   _____

   _____

   _____

B Interview three people. Use questions 1–4 in **A**. Write each person's answers in your notebook.

66 Why are you
studying English?

I'm preparing
for the TOEFL. 99

66 Is your English
improving?

My speaking is,
but my listening . . . 99

C Work with a new partner. Tell your partner about the three people you interviewed. Use (but don't read) your notes. Which answers are the most popular in your class?

66 Juan and Jin Soo are
preparing for the TOEFL.

4B GOALS   Now I can . . .

Talk about classes and school subjects _____

Talk about things I'm learning these days _____

1. Yes, I can.

2. Mostly, yes.

3. Not yet.

GLOBAL VOICES

A Watch the video. In it, four women are studying English in Chicago. Where are they from? Write the countries.

Where she's from
1. J _____
2. M _____
3. Palestine _____
4. B _____

Reason for learning English
a. She's planning to continue her education.
b. English is interesting. She always wanted to learn it.
c. She's planning to travel.
d. She needs to learn English to study nursing.
e. She's trying to communicate better and improve her skills.

B Watch the video again. Why are the women learning English? In **A**, match a person (1–4) with a reason (a–e). One reason is extra.

C Read the questions. Then watch the video one more time. Circle *Yes* or *No*.

1. Is the woman from Japan studying business? — Yes   No
2. Is the woman from Mexico studying to be a nurse? — Yes   No
3. Is the woman from Brazil planning to be a teacher? — Yes   No
4. Is the woman from Palestine planning to get a PhD in engineering? — Yes   No

D Ask and answer the questions in **C** with a partner. When you say *no*, give the correct answer.

66 Is the woman . . .?
No, she isn't. She's . . . 99

E Work with a partner.

1. **Student A:** Choose a person in **A**. Imagine you are the person.

   Student B: Ask your partner: *Why are you studying English?* Then ask one more question.

2. Change roles and repeat step 1.

66 Why are you studying English?
For my job. I'm working in . . . 99
66 Oh, is that hard?

Chicago is the third largest city in the US. It has some great universities and is known for its art scene and nightlife.

5

FOOD

LOOK AT THE PHOTO. ANSWER THE QUESTIONS.

1. Do you know the names of these foods in English?

2. Which ones do you eat?

WARM-UP VIDEO

A Read these sentences about pizza. Look up any words you don't know.

1. The main parts of pizza are dough, tomato sauce, and cheese. **T F**

2. Pizza comes from Spain. **T F**

3. Pizza is not popular in the US. **T F**

4. Pizza is popular around the world. **T F**

B What do you know about pizza? With a partner, read the sentences in **A** again. Circle **T** for *true* or **F** for *false*.

C Watch the first part of the video. Check your answers in **A**.

D Watch the video. Match the words on the left with the sentences on the right. (One item has two answers.)

1. Neapolitan pizza   a. It's white, red, and green.

2. Margherita pizza   b. It has cabbage in it.

3. the Italian flag   c. It's named after Naples.

4. lahmacun   d. It has no cheese.

5. okonomiyaki   e. It's named after a queen.

E Check the sentence that is true for you. Then discuss your answer with a partner.

☐ I like pizza a lot.

☐ Pizza is OK.

☐ I don't really like pizza.

A decoration of fruits and vegetables

GOALS

Lesson A

/ Order food from a menu

/ Talk about foods you like and dislike

Lesson B

/ Talk about healthy eating habits

/ Describe your favorite food

VOCABULARY

A Look at the photos. Listen and repeat. 🎧37

steak **and** a baked potato

spinach salad **with** tomatoes **and** onions

cheese **and** fruit

pasta **with** tomato sauce

vegetable soup **and** bread

rice **and** beans

fried chicken

a tuna fish sandwich

a burger **and** fries

B Look at the photos and the list of drinks. Answer the questions with a partner.

1. Which drinks do you like?

2. Which foods do you like?

3. What other foods and drinks do you like?

WORD BANK
Drinks
coffee
juice
soda
tea
water

The most common food truck specialties in the US are:
1. cheeseburgers, 2. tacos, 3. desserts, 4. American classics (like hot dogs), 5. sandwiches

LISTENING

A **PRONUNCIATION:** *And* Read the sentences. Listen. Notice how the word *and* is pronounced in each sentence. Then practice saying the underlined words. 🎧38

1. Your pasta comes with <u>soup and bread</u>.
2. <u>Cheese and fruit</u> is a good snack.
3. Do you want <u>a burger and fries</u>?

WORD BANK
snack

B Look at the photo and read the caption. Then answer the questions.

1. Do you and your friends eat at food trucks? How about your family?
2. What's your favorite food truck food?

C Read the information in the box. Then listen and repeat the sentences. 🎧39

1. I'd like a soda.
2. I'd like a chicken sandwich, please.
3. I'd like the salad.

ℹ️ Use *I'd like* to **order** food and drinks in a restaurant. (*I'd like* = I want)

D Lara and David are ordering from a food truck. Listen. Complete the questions. 🎧40

1. Are you ready to _____?
2. Anything to _____?
3. _____ else?

E **Listen for details.** Listen again. What do Lara and David order? Write *L* for Lara or *D* for David. 🎧40

_____ a chicken sandwich	_____ bread	_____ coffee
_____ a tuna fish sandwich	_____ fries	_____ soda
_____ pasta	_____ salad	_____ water

F Work with a partner. Practice ordering food and drinks. ❝ Are you ready to order?

Yes. I'd like the pasta, please. ❞

Pho Bo is a popular noodle soup from Vietnam.

SPEAKING

A Listen to the conversation. Then answer the questions. 🎧41

1. What kind of food is Bao asking Emily about?

2. Does she like it? What does she say?

Bao: I'm hungry.

Emily: Me, too. What do you want to eat?

Bao: Anything, really. Hey, . . . do you like (1) <u>Vietnamese</u> food?

Emily: (2) <u>I love it</u>!

Bao: I know a good restaurant near here. It's a small and (3) <u>friendly</u> place. They have good (4) <u>sandwiches and noodle soups</u>.

Emily: OK, then. Let's go!

B Practice the conversation with a partner.

C Make a new conversation in **A**.

1. Replace the words 1–4 in the conversation. Use words in the chart or your own ideas.

2. Perform your new conversation for another pair.

1	2	3	4
Chinese Italian your idea: _____	see *Speaking Strategy*	interesting popular your idea: _____	burgers pasta your idea: _____

A: Do you like Indian food?

B: It's OK, but it's not my favorite.

A: OK, then, what about Korean food?

B: I love it!

SPEAKING STRATEGY 🎧42

Talking about Likes and Dislikes

Do you like Indian food?
　I love it!
　Yeah, I like it.
　It's OK, but it's not my favorite.
　Not really.

GRAMMAR

A Read the Unit 5, Lesson A Grammar Reference in the appendix. Complete the exercises. Then do the exercises below.

THE SIMPLE PRESENT					
Affirmative Statements			**Negative Statements**		
Subject pronoun	Verb		Subject pronoun	*do / does + not*	Verb
I / You / We / They	**eat**	meat.	I / You / We / They	*don't*	**eat**	meat.
He / She / It	**eats**		He / She / It	*doesn't*	

B Read about Sylvie's habits. Complete the sentences. Use the verbs in the box. You will use some verbs more than once.

WORD BANK
breakfast
lunch
dinner

| do | drink | eat | go | know | study |

1. Sylvie _____ a glass of orange juice for breakfast. She (not) _____ coffee.

2. She _____ eggs and toast. It's her favorite.

3. After school, she _____ to a cafe and _____ her homework.

4. She _____ with friends in the library. Then they _____ dinner together.

5. Italian food is her favorite. She _____ a good place for pizza and pasta.

6. She (not) _____ there often. It's expensive.

C Write about your own habits. Complete the sentences. Use the sentences in **B** as a model. Tell a partner.

1. I ___*drink*___ _____ for breakfast. I (not) _____.

2. I _____. It's my favorite.

3. After school, I _____.

4. I _____. Then _____.

5. _____ food is my favorite. I _____ a good place for _____.

6. I _____ there often. It's _____.

Spaghetti with meatballs is a popular Italian American dish.

ACTIVE ENGLISH Try it out!

A You are having a dinner party. Read about your six dinner guests.

Mary is from London, England. She plays guitar in a band. She is Sam's girlfriend. She doesn't eat meat.

Matias is from Buenos Aires, Argentina. He lives in Canada now. He teaches music at the University of Toronto. He doesn't eat seafood.

Paula is from São Paulo, Brazil. She studies art at the University of London. She likes soccer. She eats everything!

Benny is from the Dominican Republic. He speaks English and Spanish. He plays baseball. He loves spicy food.

Sam is from LA. He's an actor. His brother lives in South America. Sam loves Italian food.

Analyn is from the Philippines. She's an actress. She speaks English, Spanish, and Tagalog. She doesn't drink soda.

B Now plan your party.

1. Think about your dinner guests' likes and dislikes. With a partner, make a menu for the party.

2. Next, think about your dinner guests' jobs and interests. Using the photo above, choose a seat at the table for each person. Include yourself and your partner at the table.

C Get together with another pair. Explain your menu and table seating.

" Here's our dinner menu. We're having . . .

Paula is in seat one. She's next to Benny. They both like sports. She's across from . . . "

5A GOALS Now I can . . .

Order food from a menu _____

Talk about foods I like and dislike _____

1. Yes, I can.
2. Mostly, yes.
3. Not yet.

VOCABULARY

A Read the six tips. Pay attention to the words in blue. Use your dictionary to help you.

1. Which tips are good? Put a check (✓).

2. Which are bad? Write *Don't* on the line.

Tips for Healthy Eating

_____ 1. Drink 6–8 glasses of water. It's **good for you**.

_____ 2. Drink a lot of soda. It's **high in** sugar.

_____ 3. Eat **healthy** snacks between **meals**.

_____ 4. Eat a lot of cake and candy. It **tastes** good, but it's **unhealthy**.

_____ 5. Eat a good breakfast. It gives you **energy**.

_____ 6. Eat a lot of food before bedtime.

WORD BANK
good for you ⟷ bad for you
high in (sugar) ⟷ low in (sugar)
healthy ⟷ unhealthy

B Check your answers in **A** with a partner. Which things (1–6) do you do?

C Answer the questions with a partner.

1. Water is good for you. What other drinks are good for you? _____

2. Soda is high in sugar. What other foods or drinks are high in sugar? _____

3. Give one example of a healthy snack. _____

4. What foods or drinks give you energy? _____

D Tell the class two of your ideas in **C**.

**Fruits and vegetables
are healthy snacks.**

TWO POWERFUL FOODS

Chili peppers are a type of fruit from the Americas. People first used them over 6,000 years ago! Today, people all over the world, from Mexico to Thailand, are using chilies in their cooking.

Chili peppers taste good, but they're also good for us. They're high in vitamin C.[1] This keeps you healthy. Many chilies are also spicy. This spice gives you energy. It also makes you less hungry, so you eat less. Doctors think chili peppers can stop some kinds of cancer, too.

Licorice, a type of plant, comes from southern Europe and Asia. Today, when people hear the word *licorice*, they think of candy. In fact, licorice is in some sweet foods (like candy) and drinks (like soda), but it is also a very old medicine.[2] Two thousand years ago, people used licorice for colds and other illnesses. Today, it is still in some cold medicines. People also use it for stomach and skin problems. Some doctors think licorice—like chili peppers—can help people with cancer! ᴴ43ᴴ

[1] *Oranges and lemons are high in* **vitamin C**.
[2] **Medicine** *is something you drink or eat to stop an illness.*

Chili peppers aren't only spicy. They're also good for you. What's another healthy food?

A Look at the photo and read the caption. Answer the question with a partner.

B Find the underlined words in your dictionary. Then answer the questions with a partner.

1. Which <u>illness</u>—<u>cancer</u> or <u>a cold</u>—is very bad?

2. Where is your <u>stomach</u>? Where is your <u>skin</u>? Point to each one.

C Read the article. Then circle your answer.

What does the article say about chilies and licorice?

a. They're both good for you.

b. Chilies are good for you, but licorice is bad for you.

c. People don't use the old foods a lot today.

D **Take notes.** Read and answer questions 1–3 about your food only.

Student A: Read about chili peppers.

Student B: Read about licorice.

1. Where does the food come from?

2. How do people use it today?

3. Why is it good for us?

E Ask a partner the questions in **D** about his or her food. What are the answers? Take notes.

F Look at your answer in **A**. Name another healthy food. Answer the questions in **D** about it. Tell a partner.

Cheese, eggs, cucumbers, and olives are part
of a typical Turkish breakfast.

LISTENING

A How many times do you have breakfast in a week? Circle your answer below. Share it with a
partner.

     a. 0   b. 1–3   c. 4–6   d. 7

B **Predict.** Students are not always healthy eaters. Read the sentences. Guess the answers. Then
listen and check your answers. 🎧44

1. You will hear the speaker talk about *skipping breakfast*. What does that mean?
To skip breakfast means to _____ _____ breakfast.

2. Skipping breakfast is _____ _____ you.

C What does the speaker say about breakfast? Read the sentences. Then listen and write your
answers. 🎧45

1. Breakfast is an important _____. It gives you a lot of _____ for the day.

2. A _____ breakfast has many different types of foods. The foods are _____
in vitamins.

D Listen again. Circle the two answers for each question. 🎧46

1. Why do students skip breakfast?

    a. They like lunch more.

    b. They're busy.

    c. It doesn't taste good.

2. How do they feel?

    a. They're tired.

    b. They're sad.

    c. They have less energy.

WORD BANK
There are three
meals in a day:
breakfast, lunch,
and dinner.

E Look at your answer in **A**. Do you have a good habit? Tell a partner.

GRAMMAR

A Read the Unit 5, Lesson B Grammar Reference in the appendix. Complete the exercises. Then do the exercises below.

YES / NO QUESTIONS				SHORT ANSWERS
Do	you they	**like**	spicy food?	Yes, I **do**. / No, I don't. Yes, they **do**. / No, they don't.
Does	he / she			Yes, he / she **does**. / No, he / she doesn't.

B Read the sentences. Add one more sentence about eating and health.

Find someone who . . .	Classmate's name
1. has a lot of energy in the morning.	
2. always eats their vegetables.	
3. takes vitamins.	
4. eats in a restaurant once a week.	
5. has coffee with breakfast.	
6. likes Chinese food.	
7. cooks simple meals.	
8. eats a healthy snack after school.	
9. likes dinner more than lunch.	
10. Your idea:	

C Play the "Find someone who" game. Ask your classmates about the information in **B**.

1. Find a different person who says *yes* to each question. Write the person's name.

2. Hurry! Complete your chart first to win the game.

66 Sae, do you have a lot of energy in the morning?　　No, I don't. 99

66 Stefan, do you have a lot of energy in the morning?　　Yes, I do! 99

Some people like to practice yoga to increase their energy.

ACTIVE ENGLISH Try it out!

A Answer the questions about your favorite food. Write your ideas in a few words.

1. What's your favorite food?
2. Where is it from?
3. When do people eat it (for breakfast, lunch, dinner, or as a snack)?

4. What's in it?
5. Is it good or bad for you? Why?

B **WRITING** Use your notes in **A** to write a paragraph about your food. Use the example to help you.

My favorite dish is paella. It's from Spain. People eat it for lunch. It has rice, chicken, seafood, onions, tomatoes, vegetables, and a spice called saffron. It's delicious and very healthy. It's high in protein, and the vegetables are good for you, too.

C Prepare a short talk about your favorite food.

1. Practice: Use your notes from **A** to talk about your food. Do not just read your paragraph.
2. Find pictures (photos, maps, etc.) or short video clips to use in your talk.

D Work in groups of four. Take turns.

1. One student: Give your talk.
   Other students: Listen and take notes. Answer the questions in **A** (*What's their favorite food? Where is it from?*).
2. After the talks, ask your group members about the different foods. Do you like them?

66 Do you like paella?

It's okay, but it's not my favorite. Do you like it? 99

66 I love it!

5B GOALS Now I can . . .

Talk about healthy eating habits _____

Describe my favorite food _____

1. Yes, I can.
2. Mostly, yes.
3. Not yet.

GLOBAL VOICES

A Write down three cities you know. What foods are they famous for? Tell a partner.

_____

_____

_____

B. Watch the first part of the video. Complete these sentences about ceviche.

1. Ceviche is a _____ dish in Peru.

2. Ceviche is very _____.

3. Many people eat ceviche for _____.

4. People eat ceviche with Peruvian _____ and _____.

C. Watch the second part of the video. Read these statements. Then circle **T** for *true* or **F** for *false*. Correct the statements that are false.

1. Abel's favorite dish is lomo saltado.   **T**   **F**

2. Lomo saltado is a typical Argentinian dish.   **T**   **F**

3. Lomo saltado is made with fish and potatoes.   **T**   **F**

4. You can have an amazing meal at world-famous and local restaurants in Lima.   **T**   **F**

D. Watch the video. Complete the task.

1. Write the ingredients from the box under each dish. One ingredient is extra.

chicken	meat	peppers	rice
lemon juice	onions	potatoes	seafood

Ceviche	Lomo saltado

2. Write a sentence like this about each food:
   Ceviche is made with _____.

E Work with a partner. Look back at your foods in **A**. Ask and answer questions about the foods.

A: . . . is famous for . . .

B: Oh really?
What's in it?

A: It's made with . . .

***Causa limeña* is a traditional Peruvian dish. It's made with potatoes, lime, and chicken or tuna.**

6

RELATIONSHIPS

LOOK AT THE PHOTO. ANSWER THE QUESTIONS.

1. How do the man and girl know each other?
2. What are they doing? Do you ever do this with your family members?

WARM-UP VIDEO

A In your country, are most families big or small?

B The video is about the Cason family. Read the sentences. Then say the numbers in each answer with your teacher.

1. The Cason family has _____ children.*

    a. 6 b. 16

2. The oldest child is _____ years old.

    a. 20 b. 22

3. The youngest child is _____ year(s) old.

    a. 1 b. 2

4. In the morning, _____ children go to four different schools.

    a. 4 b. 9

5. Sometimes, _____ children sleep in the same room.

    a. 6 b. 7

C Watch the video. Circle the correct answers in **B**.

D Answer the questions with a partner. Use ideas from the video to explain.

1. Is the Cason family big or small?
2. Is their life easy?
3. Is the family happy?
4. What do you think of the Cason family?

*1 *child* ➔ 2 *children*
kid (informal) = *child*

A man dances with his niece during a block party in New York City, US.

GOALS

Lesson A
/ Identify family members
/ Say numbers and talk about age

Lesson B
/ Talk about your relationship status
/ State relationship preferences

Sofia's Family

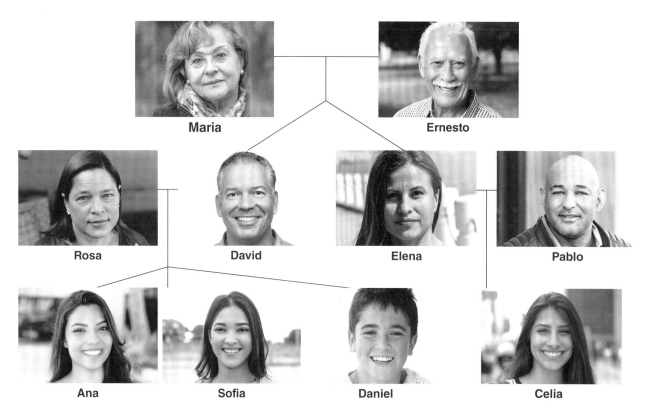

Maria   Ernesto

Rosa   David   Elena   Pablo

Ana   Sofia   Daniel   Celia

VOCABULARY

A Say the words in the Word Bank with your teacher.

B Work with a partner.

  1. Find Sofia in the family tree.

  2. Talk about her family members. Start with 1. Take turns.

    ❝ Maria is her grandmother.

C Cover the Word Bank. Who are the people in Sofia's family? Tell a partner. Take turns.

  ❝ David is her . . .

D Practice again. This time, your partner points to a person. You say the word.

E Say the words in the Word Bank with your teacher. Then find Sofia's dad in the family free. Answer the questions with a partner.

  1. Who is his wife?

  2. Who is his niece?

  3. Does he have a nephew?

WORD BANK: FAMILY

1. grandmother	8. uncle
2. grandfather	9. cousin
3. mother*	10. grandparents
4. father*	11. parents
5. sister	12. son
6. brother	13. daughter
7. aunt	

*You can also say mom and dad.

WORD BANK
husband - wife
nephew - niece

LISTENING

A Practice the numbers.

   1. Say the numbers with your teacher.

   2. Then think of five different numbers between 10 and 100. Write them in your notebook. Show a partner. He or she says the numbers.

B Look at the photo below. Answer the questions.

   1. How many children are in this family?

   2. What is the family doing?

WORD BANK: NUMBERS

10	ten	20	twenty	30	thirty
11	eleven	21	twenty-one	40	forty
12	twelve	22	twenty-two	50	fifty
13	thirteen	23	twenty-three	60	sixty
14	fourteen	24	twenty-four	70	seventy
15	fifteen	25	twenty-five	80	eighty
16	sixteen	26	twenty-six	90	ninety
17	seventeen	27	twenty-seven	100	one
18	eighteen	28	twenty-eight		hundred
19	nineteen	29	twenty-nine		

C Read sentences 1–5. Then listen. Write the correct answer. 🎧47

ℹ Saying a year
2021 twenty twenty-one
1997 nineteen ninety-seven

   1. Herman and Candelaria are from _____.

   2. The family travels together around _____.

   3. They go from place to place in a car from _____.

   4. The car is over _____ years old.
      It goes _____ kilometers per hour.

   5. In this car, the family visits different countries . . . _____ so far.

D **Listen for details.** Read sentences 1–5. Then listen. Are the <u>underlined words</u> correct? If not, change them. 🎧48

   1. The children study with <u>a teacher online</u>.

   2. They read and write, do math, and learn <u>languages</u>.

   3. The children <u>look at photos of</u> famous places.

   4. Sometimes, the family stays with Herman's <u>mother</u> in the US.

   5. The family has <u>friends</u> around the world.

E What do you think of this family's life? Is it easy? interesting? good for the children? Why? Tell a partner.

Herman and Candelaria Zapp with their children

SPEAKING

A Read and listen to the conversation. Then answer the questions. 🎧49

1. What family members does Beth talk about?

2. How old are they?

Carlos: Is someone texting you?

Beth: Yeah, my mom. Look. It's a family photo from my grandmother's birthday party.

Carlos: Nice. Is this your grandma?

Beth: Yeah. She's 85!

Carlos: That's amazing. And who's this?

Beth: My younger sister, Sonia.

Carlos: You look alike. How old is she?

Beth: Eighteen. I'm 22.

WORD BANK
grandma (*informal*) = grandmother
older ⟷ younger (brother, sister)
look alike = look the same

A teenager and her grandmother

B Practice the conversation in **A** with a partner.

C Practice again. This time, imagine Beth is talking about these people: her 80-year-old grandfather and her 19-year-old cousin, Gina.

D Find a family photo on your phone. Tell your partner about the people in the photo. Your partner will ask questions from the Speaking Strategy box.

> 66 | This is me and my cousin at Tokyo Disneyland.

> Great photo. Are you the same age? | 99

> 66 | No, my cousin is older. He's . . .

SPEAKING STRATEGY 🎧50

Talking about age

How old is your sister?
(She's) 18.
How old are you?
(I'm) 22.
Are you the same age?
Yes, we're both 20.
No, he's **older**. He's 24.
No, he's **younger**. He's 18.

E Repeat **D** with two different partners.

> 66 | These are my grandparents in 2020.

> Nice photo. How old are they now? | 99

> 66 | They're . . .

GRAMMAR

A Read the Unit 6, Lesson A Grammar Reference in the appendix. Complete the exercises. Then do the exercises below.

POSSESSIVE NOUNS	
Singular nouns	**Beth's** grandmother is 85.
Plural nouns	Her **sisters'** names are Sonia and Nadia.
Irregular plural nouns	The **men's** names are Carlos and Andres.
Names ending in -s	**Carlos's / Carlos'** family is from Peru.

B **PRONUNCIATION: Possessive 's** Listen and repeat. Then practice saying the phrases with a partner. 🎧51

my <u>sister's</u> son   <u>Beth's</u> grandmother   <u>Carlos's</u> family
the <u>boy's</u> name   my <u>parents'</u> names   Mr. <u>Gomez's</u> children

C Look at the family tree on page 76. Then complete the task.

1. Complete the questions below with the possessive.

2. Write your own question about the person.

3. Ask and answer the questions with a partner. Use the possessive in your answers.

Questions about Sofia

1. What is her (brother) ____brother's____ name?

2. What is her (sister) _____ name?

3. What are her (parents) _____ names?

4. Your question: _____

Questions about David

5. What is his (wife) _____ name?

6. What are his (daughters) _____ names?

7. What is his (niece) _____ name?

8. Your question: _____

D With a partner, research a famous person's family. It can be a real or fictional family.

1. Draw the person's family tree.

2. Talk about the family. Who are the people? Use the possessive.

A: We're talking about the family in a Korean TV show . . . Se-ri is the main character.

B: This is Se-ri's father. He loves his daughter. But Se-ri's stepmother . . .

E Get together with another pair. Talk about your family in **D**. At the end, ask the other pair four questions. What do they remember?

❝ What are her older brothers' names?

ACTIVE ENGLISH Try it out!

A Work with a partner.

Student A: Turn to page 213.

Student B: Work on your own. Read 1–10 below. Write the answers.

Questions to ask your partner

In English, what's the word for your . . .

1. mother's mother? _____

2. father's sister? _____

3. uncle's son? _____

4. own female child? _____

Do the math.

5. What is 15 + 15? _____

6. What is 37 + 22? _____

7. What is 100 – 25? _____

8. What is 80 – 67? _____

Talk about your family.

9. Who is the oldest person in your family? How old is the person?

10. Who is your favorite family member? What is the person's name and how old is he or she?

WORD BANK

+ plus
– minus

oldest
youngest

B Work with your partner. To do this exercise, you need a timer. Follow the steps. If you don't know an answer, say *pass*.

1. One person goes first. Start the timer.

2. Ask your partner your questions in **A** (1–10). Your partner answers quickly. Check (✓) the answers your partner says correctly.

3. At the end, write your partner's total time and the number of correct answers.

4. Change roles and repeat steps 2 and 3.

C Compare your scores. Who did better: you or your partner?

D On your own, create your own quiz of 10 items (like the one in **A**).

E Work with your partner again. Repeat **B** and **C**.

6A GOALS Now I can . . .

Identify family members _____

Say numbers and talk about age _____

1. Yes, I can.
2. Mostly, yes.
3. Not yet.

VOCABULARY

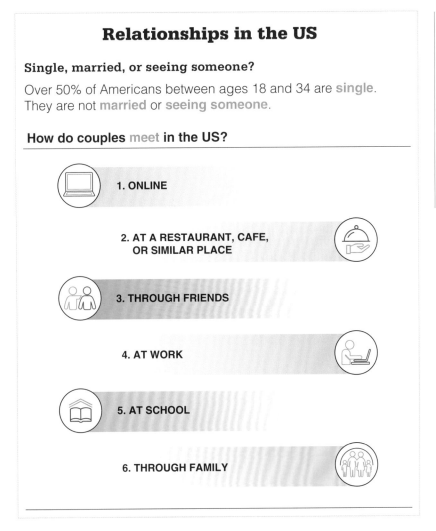

Relationships in the US

Single, married, or seeing someone?

Over 50% of Americans between ages 18 and 34 are single. They are not married or seeing someone.

How do couples meet in the US?

1. ONLINE

2. AT A RESTAURANT, CAFE, OR SIMILAR PLACE

3. THROUGH FRIENDS

4. AT WORK

5. AT SCHOOL

6. THROUGH FAMILY

WORD BANK

I'm	single.	
He's	married.	
She's	seeing someone.	
My	husband's	
His	wife's	name
Her	boyfriend's	is . . .
	girlfriend's	

A couple is two people. They are married or seeing each other.

A Say the words in the Word Bank with your teacher, and talk about their meanings.

B Read the information above. Answer the questions with a partner.

1. Are most people between 18 and 34 seeing someone?
2. What are the top three ways people in the US meet others?
3. Are these things true in your country?

66 In my country, most people meet . . .

C Complete the chart. Write about yourself and two people you know. Then share your answers with a partner. Are these people similar to people in the US?

Person	Age	Single, married, or seeing someone?	They met . . .
1.			
2.			
3.			

present	past
meet	→ met

TIME TO GET MARRIED?

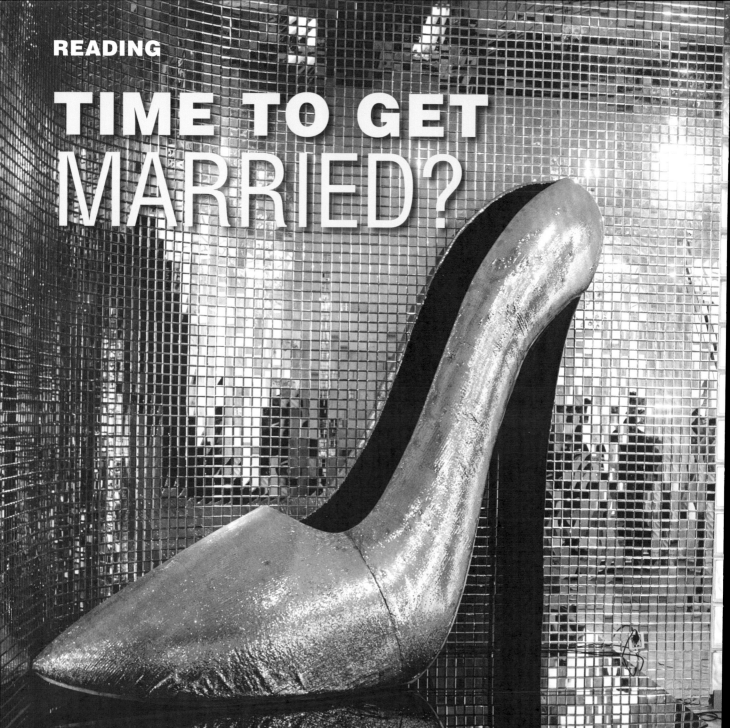

Song Zongpei[1] lives in Beijing, China. Her life and her mother's are very different. At 28, Ms. Song's mother was[2] married with a child. Today, Ms. Song is 28. She's got a job and lives in her own apartment with two roommates. She's also single, and—as she told *The New York Times*—she has no plans to get married soon or have a family.

Ms. Song isn't alone. Today in China, fewer[3] people are getting married, especially in big cities. One recent study, for example, interviewed a large group of people in Shanghai. Almost 10% say they are planning to stay single. They don't want to get married now or in the future. Others are waiting until their thirties[4] to get married.

Some parents don't like these changes. They want their children to find someone and get married by age 28 or 29. This is the way to a happy life, the parents say. But more single people don't agree with this idea. They're happy now. Married life, they say, can wait. 🎧 52

[1] *Song is the woman's family name. In China, a person's family name comes first.*
[2] **Was** *is the past form of* is.
[3] **Fewer** *means a smaller number of something.*
[4] **thirties:** *ages 30–39*

A couple in China takes wedding photos. But in this country, fewer people are getting married these days.

A Read the sentences in the box below. Then tell a partner: In your opinion, is there a good age to get married (25, 30, 35)? Explain.

> (adjective) He is **married**.
> (verb) Many people **get married** every year.

B **Skim for the gist.** Look at the photo and read the caption and the title of the article. Guess: What is the reading's main idea? Circle the best answer.

These days in China, more people _____.

a. don't have money to get married

b. are staying single

c. are not happy with their wife or husband

C Read the article to check your answer in **B**.

D Read sentences 1–7. Circle **T** for *true* or **F** for *false*. Correct the false sentences so they are true.

1. At 28, Ms. Song's mother was single.   T   F

2. Today, Ms. Song, 28, lives with her parents.   T   F

3. Ms. Song is seeing someone.   T   F

4. She doesn't plan to get married soon.   T   F

5. There are more single people in big cities in China.   T   F

6. In cities, more people are getting married at age 28.   T   F

7. Many single people in China are not happy.   T   F

E Answer the questions. Compare your ideas with a partner's.

1. Look at your answer in **B**. In your opinion, why is this happening? Think of one or two reasons.

2. Read the last paragraph again. What do some parents want and why? Do you agree with these parents? Why or why not?

LISTENING

A Look at the graph. What does it show? Tell a partner.

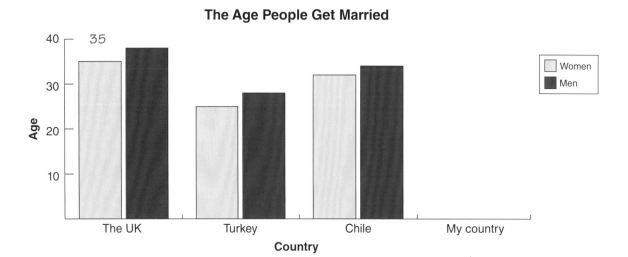

The Age People Get Married

Legend: Women (light), Men (dark)

X-axis (Country): The UK, Turkey, Chile, My country
Y-axis (Age): 10, 20, 30, 40

(The UK: Women 35, Men ~38; Turkey: Women ~25, Men ~28; Chile: Women ~32, Men ~34)

B **Listen for details.** Listen to the first part of an interview. Write the ages above the bars in **A**. 🎧53

WORD BANK
in (your) twenties
= ages 20–29

This couple married after seven years together.

C Listen again. Complete the sentence with the best answer. 🎧53

In some countries, people are getting married _____.

a. younger

b. later

c. more than one time

D Listen to the rest of the interview. Write a word in each blank. 🎧54

Reasons for the change

1. More people—especially _____— are going to _____.

2. Men and women have got _____. They are thinking about _____ and _____, not about getting married.

E Answer the questions with a partner.

1. Is your country similar to the countries in the chart? Look online and add the ages.

2. Look at your answers in **D**. Are these things true in your country? Give examples.

GRAMMAR

A Read the Unit 6, Lesson B Grammar Reference in the appendix. Complete the exercises. Then do the exercises below.

HAVE GOT			
I've / You've / We've / They've	got	a good job. a nice apartment a big family. a lot of free time.	I've got = I have got He's got = He has got
He's / She's			

B Circle the things in the box that you have. Then compare answers with a partner.

a boyfriend or girlfriend	a cousin	a pet
a brother or sister	a hobby	a phone
a college degree	a job	a small family

> **i** You can use *have got* or *have*. They mean the same thing.

A: Do you have a brother?

B: No, I don't. I've got a sister.

A: Oh? How old is she?

B: 19. We're twins! What about you?

A: I've got a sister, too, but she's younger.

C Which things do you and your partner both have? Tell another pair.

> " We've both got sisters. Lena's sister is 19. My sister is 18.

D Which things does everyone in your group have? Tell the class.

> We've all got sisters but they're different ages. "

Are there any twins in your class?

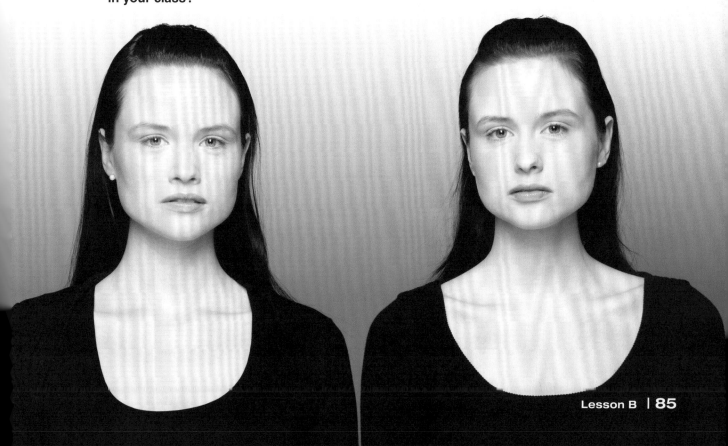

ACTIVE ENGLISH Try it out!

A Review the survey with the class. Then work on your own. Choose your answers.

What's important to you in a partner?*	
1. He's got / She's got . . . (Choose three.) ☐ a college degree. ☐ a lot of money. ☐ the same hobbies and interests. ☐ a nice family. ☐ a handsome / beautiful face. ☐ a great personality. (He or she is friendly.) ☐ a good job. ☐ my idea: _____	**2. He / She is . . .** ☐ older. ☐ the same age. ☐ younger. ☐ A person's age isn't important to me. **3. He / She . . .** ☐ is from the same country. ☐ wants to get married. ☐ other: _____

*Your (**romantic**) **partner** is your husband, wife, boyfriend, or girlfriend.

B Work in a small group. Share your answers. Explain your reasons.

> 66 For number 1, my answer is "He's got . . ."

C Now answer the questions together.

1. Are men's and women's answers similar or different?
2. What answers from **A** are the most common in your group?
   Tell another group.

D Read about the two people.

1. Look at the underlined words. Are they correct? If not, change them.
2. Answer the questions with a partner.
   - How old is each person?
   - Are they single, married, or seeing someone?

In my country, many people get married in their <u>twenty</u>. In my case, <u>I have 22 years</u>. I'm single and I like it. I'm going to college, and <u>I've got</u> a lot of friends. I don't want a relationship* right now.	In my country, many people get married at 29 or 30. In my case, <u>I'm 26</u>. <u>I'm see someone</u>, but we don't want to get married right now. These days, I'm preparing for job interviews. My boyfriend <u>is 28</u>. <u>He got</u> an important job in a big hotel. We're busy.

*"I don't want a relationship" means "I don't want a romantic partner."

E **WRITING** Write five or six sentences about yourself. Use the examples in **D** to help you.

6B GOALS Now I can . . .

Talk about my relationship status _____

State relationship preferences _____

1. Yes, I can.
2. Mostly, yes.
3. Not yet.

GLOBAL VOICES

A Read the sentences below. Then watch the video. Circle the correct answers.

Miyri
1. She's got **four** / **five** brothers and **one sister** / **no sisters**.
2. She is **single** / **married**.

Abel
3. He's got **a sister** / **two sisters**.
4. His mother's **sister** / **mother** lives with his family.

Lizzy
5. Her brother is **24** / **25**.
6. Her sister is **12** / **20**. She's **younger** / **older**.

Dickie
7. He's got **a brother** / **two brothers**.
8. **Dickie** / **Dickie's brother** is married.

Max
9. He is **single** / **married**.
10. He has **a child** / **no children**.

B With a partner, ask and answer the questions about the people in **A**.

1. Who's married?
2. Who's a parent?
3. Who has both brothers *and* sisters? How old are they?
4. Who lives with a grandparent?

C Read sentences 1–4. Then watch and circle *true* or *false*. Correct the false answers.

1. A lot of Marcel's family members live in the same building.   True   False
2. Ricardo's parents are from China.   True   False
3. Abel's mother makes movies and TV commercials.   True   False
4. David is from Israel. His parents are from Morocco.   True   False

WORD BANK
A *building* is a large place to live or work.

D Now it's your turn. In your notebook, describe your family. Then explain:

What is something interesting about your family or one of your family members?

E Work with a partner. Follow the steps.

1. For one minute, talk about your family. Don't use your notes. When you listen, ask questions.
2. Repeat step 1 with two other people.

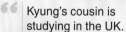
" My cousin lives in the UK.

Is he a student? "

F Tell the class one fact about your partner's family.

" Kyung's cousin is studying in the UK.

Families at Yoyogi Park in Tokyo, Japan

Empanadas are popular in many Latin American countries. They're made with different ingredients in each region. This is a corn *empanada*.

A Do you read or watch restaurant reviews?

B A woman is vlogging* about her favorite restaurant. 🎧55

1. Read her comments below. Pay attention to the <u>underlined words</u>.

2. Listen. Are the underlined words correct? If not, change them.

WORD BANK
In a restaurant review, a person gives an opinion about a restaurant or other place to eat.

Today, my friend and I are eating <u>dinner</u> at our favorite <u>Mexican</u> restaurant: Carla's Kitchen. It's Carla Mendoza and her <u>husband's</u> restaurant. Their <u>sons</u> work there, too.

The restaurant is famous for a <u>chicken</u> dish called *pollo a la brasa*. To make it, Carla uses her <u>grandmother's</u> recipe. This really is a family business! Many people order the <u>steak</u>, but the menu has got lots of other things, too.

*Vlogging** means posting videos online.

C Read items 1 and 2. Then listen and complete the tasks. 🎧56

1. Complete each person's meal with the words in the box. Two words are extra.

beans	chicken	onions	a salad	steak
cheese	fries	rice	spinach	tomatoes

The woman is having the _____ dish. It comes with _____ and _____.

Her friend is eating *empanadas*. The beef empanada has got _____, _____, and _____ in it. The vegetable empanada has got _____ and _____ inside.

2. Write the numbers.

Total for the meal: $_____

For each person: $_____

D Do you like the food at Carla's Kitchen? Complete an expression and tell a partner why.

Yeah, I . . .　　　　It's OK, but . . .　　　　Not . . .

E Think of your favorite place to eat. Complete the information.

The place's name: _____

Type of food: _____

Location: _____

Popular dish(es): _____

> **Places to eat**
> a restaurant
> a cafe
> a food truck or stall
> a family member's home
> your idea: _____

F **You Choose** Go to your favorite place to eat. Choose an option. Then follow the instructions in the box.

Option 1: Make a video of the place and the food.

Option 2: Make a podcast about the place and the food. Record your opinions.

Option 3: Give a presentation about the place and the food. Take photos and write sentences about them.

" My favorite place is in Shinchon subway station. It doesn't have a name. It's a food stall. In this photo, I'm eating . . .

" My favorite place to eat is my aunt's house. Today, she's making . . . "

> **At the start of your review:**
> Greet people.
> Talk about the information in **E**.
>
> **Then explain:**
> Are you having a snack or a meal?
> What are you eating or drinking? Talk about it.
> How's the food? Do you like it?
> Is the place expensive?

G Work with a partner. Watch, listen to, or read your partner's review.

1. Ask your partner questions.

" In the video, what are you drinking? It looks good.

2. Explain: Do you like your partner's place? Why or why not?

" Yeah, I like it, and I want to go!

It's OK, but pizza isn't my favorite food. "

7

TIME

LOOK AT THE PHOTO. ANSWER THE QUESTIONS.

1. Say the days of the week with your teacher.

Monday	**Friday**
Tuesday	**Saturday**
Wednesday	**Sunday**
Thursday	

Which one is your favorite?

2. When is the weekend in your country? Say the day(s).

WARM-UP VIDEO

A Watch the first 40 seconds of the video. How does Carlos feel? Circle your answer.

happy   nervous   relaxed

B Watch the video. What do we know about Carlos? Write *T* for *true*, *F* for *false*, or *?* for *don't know*.

1. _____ It's 8:45.
2. _____ Carlos lives with his family.
3. _____ He's from Canada.
4. _____ Carlos has a big breakfast.
5. _____ He's taking a business class.
6. _____ Today is Friday.

C Look up the word *late* in your dictionary. Then answer the question. Explain your answer to a partner.

Is Carlos late for work?

_____

D When you are late, how do you feel? Tell a partner.

The Prague Astronomical Clock is an old and beautiful clock. It's popular with locals and tourists.

GOALS

Lesson A

/ Tell time and describe your daily routine

/ Make and respond to suggestions

Lesson B

/ Talk about weekend activities

/ Ask and answer information questions

VOCABULARY

A Say the times on the clocks with your teacher. Then work with a partner.

1. Cover the words. Point at a clock.
2. Ask your partner, *What time is it?*

half   a quarter

It's one o'clock.

It's one-fifteen.
It's a quarter past one.

It's one thirty.
It's half past one.

It's one forty-five.
It's a quarter to two.

B Read about Max's day. Then tell a partner about it.

Max wakes up at 6:30 and has breakfast.

Then he takes a shower and gets dressed.

He leaves home at 7:30 and goes to school.

His classes start at 8:15 and finish at 3:45.

He goes home at 4:00.

He goes to bed at 10:30.

C Use the words in blue in **B** to tell your partner about your daily routine.

“ I wake up at 5:30.
That's early! ”

WORD BANK
early ⟷ late

LISTENING

A Look at the photo and read the caption. Where is the astronaut? What is he doing?

B Life on the International Space Station is busy. Listen to an astronaut's daily schedule. Follow the steps. 🎧57

WORD BANK

in the { morning / afternoon / evening

1. Read the list of activities.

2. Do astronauts do these activities in the morning (M), afternoon (A), or evening (E)? Check (✓) your answers.

	M	A	E
exercise			
get dressed			
leave the space station			
talk on the phone			
watch movies			
work on science projects			

C **Listen for numbers.** Listen again. Write the times astronauts do these activities. 🎧57

1. wake up _____
2. have lunch _____
3. start working again _____
4. exercise _____
5. go to bed _____

D In your opinion, is life on the International Space Station interesting? Why or why not?

Astronaut Franklin R. Chang-Diaz on a spacewalk outside the International Space Station. Behind him is Earth.

SPEAKING

A PRONUNCIATION: Numbers Listen and repeat. Notice the different stress. 🎧58

1. The movie starts at 8:<u>15</u>.
2. The movie starts at 8:<u>50</u>.
3. Class finishes at 3:<u>13</u>.
4. Class finishes at 3:<u>30</u>.

B Listen to the conversation. Read the sentences and circle **T** for *true* or **F** for *false*. 🎧59

1. Jon likes action movies.	T	F
2. Bong Joon Ho is an actor.	T	F
3. Mindy likes Bong Joon Ho.	T	F
4. Mindy wants to go at 11:30.	T	F

Jon: Let's go to the park.

Mindy: But it's too cold outside.

Jon: We could see a movie.

Mindy: Great idea. How about an action movie?

Jon: I don't like action movies. We could see the new Bong Joon Ho movie.

Mindy: That's a good idea. He's my favorite director. What time does it start?

Jon: There's a show at 8:15 and one at 11:30.

Mindy: 11:30 is late. Let's go to the early show.

Jon: Sounds good!

A movie theater in Los Angeles, USA

C Look at the conversation again. How do Jon and Mindy make suggestions? Find two examples. Underline them. Practice the conversation.

D Use the Speaking Strategy to complete the conversation. Then practice with a partner.

A: What do you want to do after class?

B: _____ play video games.

A: _____ video games.

SPEAKING STRATEGY 🎧60
Making and responding to suggestions

Making a suggestion	Saying *yes*	Saying *no* politely
Let's go to the park. We could see a movie. How about an action movie?	(That's a) good idea. (That's a) great idea. (That) sounds good.	I don't really like action movies.

B: OK, well, _____ see a movie.

A: _____. What do you want to see?

E Add three or four more lines to the conversation in **D**.

Student B: Suggest a movie to see.

Student A: You don't want to see Student B's movie. Suggest another idea.

Students A & B: Agree on a movie and a time to see it.

GRAMMAR

A Read the Unit 7, Lesson A Grammar Reference in the appendix. Complete the exercises. Then do the exercises below.

PREPOSITIONS OF TIME	

When's your class?
    It's **at** 8:30.
    It's **in** the morning.
    It's **on** Monday.
    It's **from** 4:00 **to** 5:30.
    It's **from** Monday **to** Friday.
	Use *when* to ask about times and days.
	Use *at* for an exact time.
	Use *in* for a period of time.
	Use *on* for days of the week.
	Use *from . . . to* for start and finish times.

i Notice:
in the evening
but *at* night

B Do you remember the days of the week? Say them with your teacher.

Monday	Tuesday	Wednesday	Thursday	Friday	Saturday	Sunday

C Follow these steps.

1. Write the missing words.

2. Read the pairs of sentences. For the second sentence in each pair, circle *True*, *False*, or *Don't know*.

1. Their party is _____ the evening.
It lasts for two hours.   True   False   Don't know

2. The party is _____ Saturday.
It's not _____ the weekend.   True   False   Don't know

3. My English class is _____ 9:30.
It starts at 9:30.   True   False   Don't know

4. It's _____ 9:30 _____ 10:15.
It last for 45 minutes.   True   False   Don't know

D Read the sentences. Correct the errors. Some sentences are correct.

1. My schedule is hard. I work at the night. My work hours are at 10:00 to 6:00.

2. My classes start the afternoon. The first class is on 2:00.

3. My birthday is on Tuesday this year. Luckily, we don't have classes in my birthday.

E Complete the sentences with your own information.

1. I like to study _____ the **morning / afternoon / evening**.

2. I do most of my homework _____ **school days / Saturdays and Sundays**.

3. My favorite subject is _____. The class starts _____ _____*.

4. My birthday is _____ _____** this year.

    *Write in a time here.   **Write in a day of the week here.

F Take turns. Ask a partner about the information in **E**.

  66 When do you like
    to study?
            In the
        afternoon. 99

Students prepare for a test in China.

ACTIVE ENGLISH Try it out!

A Work with a partner. Follow the steps.

Student A: Read the directions on this page.

Student B: Turn to page 214. Read the directions there.

STUDENT A

- Look at the activities in your schedule below. Don't show your schedule to Student B.

- Task 1: You're taking a big test on Friday afternoon at 4:00. You want to study with your partner for two hours to prepare for the test. Find a good time to study together.

- Task 2: You want to see a movie at 7:00 in the evening. Find a good day to go.

> Discuss your Wednesday schedules first. Then look at your Thursday and Friday schedules. Use these expressions: *Are you free...?*   *I'm busy.*

My schedule

	Wednesday	Thursday	Friday
1:00		eat lunch	in class
2:00	eat lunch		in class
3:00			
4:00			take a test
5:00	play soccer		
6:00	do homework	shop with friends	
7:00		do homework	

Student A: Let's study together for the test.

Student B: Good idea!

Student A: Are you free on Wednesday at 3:00?

Student B: I'm sorry, but I'm busy then. I'm in class. How about 5:00?

B Think of your own idea for Saturday or Sunday. Make a plan with your partner.

7A GOALS   Now I can . . .

Tell time and describe my daily routine _____

Make and respond to suggestions _____

1. Yes, I can.
2. Mostly, yes.
3. Not yet.

VOCABULARY

A Complete the chart. Use the words in the box.

biking	driving	friend's house	movies	run

go + *-ing* verb	*go for* + an activity	*go to* + a place or event
go running	go for a _____	go to a concert
go _____	go for a bike ride	go to a _____
go _____	go for a drive	go to the _____

B Read the list and write the missing words. Then check (✓) the activities you do on the weekend.

1. ☐ _____ a cafe
2. ☐ _____ a walk
3. ☐ _____ the beach
4. ☐ _____ shopping
5. ☐ _____ a park

6. ☐ _____ a picnic
7. ☐ _____ swimming
8. ☐ _____ a hike
9. ☐ _____ dancing
10. ☐ _____ a mall

WORD BANK
weekend

C Tell a partner about your answers in **B**. Are your weekends similar or different?

Governors Island sits in New York Harbor. There are no cars there, so it's a great place to go for a bike ride.

READING

WHAT TYPE OF
WEEKEND
PERSON ARE YOU?

Most people work during the week and have fun on the weekend. The weekend is a good time to go for a walk, go shopping, or just hang out with friends. Not everyone relaxes on the weekend, though. Different people enjoy the weekend in different ways.

Read about these four types of people. What type of weekend person are you?

THE COUCH POTATO

What's your perfect weekend? Sleeping late, watching TV, and playing video games. Some people are busy on the weekend, but not you! You're happy to stay on the couch all day.

THE WORKAHOLIC

You're always busy: working, studying, talking on the phone, or checking emails. When you go out with friends on the weekend, you're thinking about your work or your next exam.

A **Use key words to predict.** The article is about four types of people. Look at the photos. Then answer the question.

Who relaxes and does nothing on the weekend? Guess. Write a check (✓) next to your answer(s).

Key words

1. ☐ the couch potato _____
   _____

2. ☐ the health nut _____

3. ☐ the party animal _____
   _____

4. ☐ the workaholic _____

B Read the article. Check your answer in **A**. Write 3–4 key words about each type of person.

C Now compare your answers with a partner.

THE HEALTH NUT

You want to get busy and do things! You usually wake up early (yes, even on the weekend) and go for a walk, a run, or a bike ride. All week, you're sitting and looking at a computer screen. On the weekend, it's time to exercise!

THE PARTY ANIMAL

For you, the weekend is all about fun—and lots of it. Your night starts at 9:00 or 10:00. You go dancing or go to a party with friends. Then you go home late at night and sleep late the next day. Then you wake up in the afternoon and do it all again!

D Read the article again. Match the people on the left to the activities on the right.

1. the couch potato
2. the health nut
3. the party animal
4. the workaholic

a. check emails
b. go dancing
c. go for a run
d. go to a party
e. play video games
f. sleep late
g. wake up early
h. work

E What type of weekend person are you? Check (✓) your answer.

☐ a couch potato

☐ a health nut

☐ a party animal

☐ a workaholic

☐ a mix of two types:
the _____
and the _____

F Explain your answer to a partner.

LISTENING

A Look at the photo. Where are the people? What are they doing?

B **Listen for main points.** Read the sentences and guess the answers. Then listen and check your answers. 🎧62🎧

1. The main activity at Daybreaker is **eating** / **dancing**.
2. It finishes at **6:00** / **9:00** in the **morning** / **evening**.
3. It **is** / **isn't** on the weekend.

C Listen again. Complete the sentences. 🎧62🎧

1. Kim is going _____.
2. Daybreaker lasts for _____ hours.
3. Everyone is dancing _____.
4. People drink _____ to stay awake.
5. After the party, the people go to _____.
6. They feel _____ and have more energy.

D Answer the questions with a partner.

1. What things do you see at a Daybreaker party?

   ☐ a DJ   ☐ smiling people   ☐ tired dancers   ☐ unhealthy snacks

2. What type of person doesn't enjoy Daybreaker parties? Explain your answer.

   | a couch potato | a health nut | a party animal |

3. Do you want to go to a Daybreaker party? Why or why not?

Taking a break and having fun at a party

GRAMMAR

A Read the Unit 7, Lesson B Grammar Reference in the appendix. Complete the exercises. Then do the exercises below.

THE SIMPLE PRESENT: *WH-* QUESTIONS					Short answers
Question word	*do / does*	Subject	Main verb		
Where	do	you	go	on the weekend?	*Where do you go on the weekend?*
What	does	she	do	after school?	*To the park.*
When	do	classes	start?		*The park.*
Who	do	you	study	with?	

B Read Ava's Saturday schedule. Unscramble questions 1–4. Start each item with a question word. Then ask and answer the questions with a partner.

> **On Saturday, Ava . . .**
> * works in an office from 9:00 to 3:30.
> * goes to the gym in the afternoon.
> * goes out with her friends at night.

1. Ava / work / does / when

   _____ ?

2. does / work / where / she

   _____ ?

3. she / what / do / in the afternoon / does

   _____ ?

4. who / at night / Ava / does / go out with

   _____ ?

C Cover up **B**. Read Ava's Sunday schedule. Write four questions about it. Then ask and answer the questions with a partner.

> **On Sunday, Ava . . .**
> * wakes up at 10:00.
> * goes for a bike ride in the park in the afternoon.
> * studies with her classmates in the evening.

1. (when) _____
2. (what) _____
3. (where) _____
4. (who) _____

D Complete the sentences about a classmate.

1. He / She lives _____ .
2. He / She lives with _____ .
3. He / She studies with _____ .
4. He / She goes _____ on the weekend.

E Ask a partner about his or her classmate. Listen to the answers. Can you guess the person's name?

ACTIVE ENGLISH Try it out!

A Use the question words in the box. Complete the six questions.

what	when	where	who

1. _____ do you go for a walk?
2. _____ do you do for fun?
3. _____ do you study with?
4. _____ do you live?
5. _____ do you talk with your friends about?
6. _____ do you do your homework?

B Work with a partner. Ask and answer the questions in **A**.

C **WRITING** Work with the same partner. Write your own six questions. Use the verbs in **A** or your own ideas.

Example: **When do you wake up?**

1. _____
2. _____
3. _____
4. _____
5. _____
6. _____

D Join another pair to play a memory game. Students A and B are one team. Students C and D are another team.

1. Student A asks Student C all six questions from **C**. Student C answers. Student B listens closely, but doesn't write anything down.

   Examples: When do you wake up? / I wake up at 7:00.
   What do you watch on TV? / I watch dramas.

2. How many answers can Student B remember? Now Student A asks the six questions again to Student B.

   Examples: When does she wake up? / She wakes up at 7:00.
   What does she watch on TV? / I can't remember!

E Play the game again.

1. This time Student C asks his or her questions from **C**. Student A answers. Student D listens and has to remember the answers. Follow the same steps in **D**.

2. Keep playing until every student gets a chance to ask questions.

7B GOALS Now I can . . .

Talk about weekend activities _____

Ask and answer information questions _____

1. Yes, I can.
2. Mostly, yes.
3. Not yet.

GLOBAL VOICES

A In the video, people answer the two questions below. Guess what things they say. Tell a partner.

1. What do you do on the weekend?
2. What is your typical day* like?

*Your **typical day** means *what you do every day*.

B What do people do on the weekend? Watch the video. Circle **T** for *true* or **F** for *false*.

1. Meki goes out with her friends.	**T**	**F**
2. Meki and her family watch movies and play sports.	**T**	**F**
3. Isabel goes swimming every weekend.	**T**	**F**
4. Lingo doesn't like to sleep.	**T**	**F**
5. For vacation, he likes to go to the beach.	**T**	**F**

C Read the lists. There is one extra item in each list. Watch the video. Cross out the extra item.

My typical day	
Isabel	**Mireille**
_____ get dressed	_____ go to school
_____ go to sleep[1]	_____ go to the gym
_____ go to work	_____ hang out with[3] friends
_____ wake up	_____ have breakfast
_____ watch TV	_____ have dinner
_____ work out[2]	_____ wake up

[1]**Go to sleep** means *go to bed*.
[2]**Work out** means *exercise*.
[3]**Hang out with** means *spend time with*.

D Watch again. What are Isabel and Mireille's typical days like? Put the items in **C** in order from 1 to 5.

E Ask and answer the questions in **A** with a partner.

In some countries, like Cuba and Brazil, people play dominoes every week and, even, every day!

In November, people in Mexico remember family members on the Day of the Dead. Sometimes, there are parades and people dress up in costumes, too.

GOALS

Lesson A

/ Talk about important dates

/ Say you know or don't know something

Lesson B

/ State when and how long an event is

/ Describe what happens at a festival

8

SPECIAL OCCASIONS

LOOK AT THE PHOTO. ANSWER THE QUESTIONS.

1. The women in the photo are dressed up for the Day of the Dead. When and where does it happen?

2. What happens on the Day of the Dead?

WARM-UP VIDEO

A Look up the words in your dictionary. What do you think the video is about?

cello	ice
festival	instrument

B Read the sentences. Look up any words you don't know in a dictionary. Then watch the video. Circle the correct answers.

1. This happens in **Norway** / **Iceland**.

2. They **play** / **sell** ice instruments.

3. It looks like his real **piano** / **cello**.

4. The man plays music for five **minutes** / **hours**.

5. The music **is** / **isn't** beautiful.

6. They play music in a **cool** / **cold** place.

7. The ice goes to a **ski** / **big** village.

8. They **make** / **cut** the ice.

C Use the words in the box to complete the sentences. Do you like cold places? Do you like ice music?

cold	instruments	music
ice	listen	village

1. Norway is a _____ place.

2. They have an ice _____ festival there.

3. People take _____ to a ski

   _____.

4. They make _____ from the ice.

5. People like to _____ to the music.

VOCABULARY

A Practice saying the months and seasons of the year with a partner. Then write the name of the season next to the correct month for your country.

Month	Season	Special occasion
January		
February		
March		
April		
May		
June		
July		
August		
September		
October		
November		
December		

winter
spring
summer
fall

WORD BANK
There are four **weeks** in a **month**.
There are twelve **months** in a **year**.

B Work with a partner.

1. In two minutes, name as many holidays and festivals as you can.

2. Write each one next to the correct month.

3. Tell another pair about your list. Which ones are your favorites?

The Yi Peng Festival is in November.

Is it your favorite?

At the Yi Peng Festival in Chiang Mai, Thailand, people light lanterns and make wishes.

The Monument to the Revolution in Mexico City

LISTENING

A **Pronunciation: Ordinal numbers** Look at the dates. Notice how we write them. Practice saying the dates with a partner. Then listen and repeat the dates and ordinal numbers. 🎧63

How to *write* dates	How to *say* dates
January 1	January first
September 2	September second
July 23	July twenty-third
July 30	July thirtieth

first	sixth	twentieth
second	seventh	thirtieth
third	eighth	
fourth	ninth	
fifth	tenth	

B **Listen for spelling.** Pedro is flying home for summer vacation. Listen and write his last name. Then circle the correct answers. 🎧64

Last name: ____ ____ ____ ____ ____

First name: P E D R O

1. Where is he now? Las Vegas Mexico City Vancouver

2. Where is he going to? Las Vegas Mexico City Vancouver

WORD BANK
return

C **Listen for dates.** What is Pedro's schedule? Listen and complete the chart. 🎧65

	Old dates	New dates
Leaving		
Returning		

D Listen and complete the sentences. 🎧66

1. I want to make a _____.

2. Yes, that's _____.

3. Yes, with your _____, that's fine.

4. That _____ isn't good.

5. Those days are less _____.

6. Have a _____ trip, Mr. Lopez.

E Answer the questions with a partner.

1. Look at the new dates in **C**. Are these good dates to travel in your country?

2. What are the best months to travel in your country?

On St. Patrick's Day, everyone wears green.

SPEAKING

i *St.* is pronounced "saint."

A Skim the conversation. Circle any words you don't know. Look them up in your dictionary.

Tony: It's so crowded!

Lena: And look! There's a parade over there.

Tony: Is today a holiday?

Lena: I'm not sure. Let me check my phone. OK, it says it's St. Patrick's Day . . .

Tony: St. Patrick's Day? What's that?

Lena: I have no idea. Let me see . . . It says, "St. Patrick's Day is on March 17."

Tony: That's today.

Lena: It also says, "On St. Patrick's Day, people celebrate all things Irish."

Tony: Well, it looks like fun. Come on, let's watch the parade!

B Listen to the conversation in **A**. Then answer the questions. 🎧 67

1. What happens on St. Patrick's Day?   2. When is it?

C Practice the conversation in **A** with a partner.

D Answer the questions below with a partner. Use the Speaking Strategy to help you.

1. When is Mexico's Independence Day?
   a. May 5
   b. August 24
   c. September 16
2. Where is the New Year called *Hogmanay*?
   a. in Russia
   b. in Scotland
   c. in Iceland

3. Where does Children's Day happen on May 5?
   a. in Italy and Greece
   b. in Chile and Peru
   c. in Korea and Japan
4. What holiday is on October 31 in the United States?
   a. Halloween
   b. Thanksgiving
   c. Christmas

> **SPEAKING STRATEGY** 🎧 68
> **Saying you know or don't know something**
>
> Is today a holiday?
>
> | Yes, it is. / No, it isn't. | (certain) |
> | Maybe. | (less certain) |
> | I'm not sure. | (not certain at all) |
> | I don't know. | (don't know) |
> | I have no idea. | |

" Where is the New Year called *Hogmanay*? Is it in Russia?

I don't know. What do you think? "

E Check your answers on page 217. Who has the most correct answers in your class?

GRAMMAR

A Read the Unit 8, Lesson A Grammar Reference in the appendix. Complete the exercises. Then do the exercises below.

WH- QUESTIONS WITH PREPOSITIONS	
St. Patrick's Day is <u>on</u> Saturday. 　**What day is St. Patrick's Day <u>on</u>?** The parade is <u>at</u> 11:00. 　**What time is the parade <u>at</u>?** I live <u>in</u> Brazil. 　**What country do you live <u>in</u>?** She lives <u>with</u> her parents. 　**Who does she live <u>with</u>?** He listens <u>to</u> hip-hop. 　**What kind of music does he listen <u>to</u>?**	Many sentences have verbs followed by prepositions. When we make question forms for those sentences, the preposition moves to the end of the sentence.

B Look at the photo. Read about the Namahage festival in Japan. What do people do in the festival? Write a sentence about it.

In the Namahage Festival, _____.

The Namahage festival happens in Oga City, Japan in December.
In the festival, men put on a *namahage* costume.
They go to different houses in the city.
They're looking for naughty* children.

At each house, they ask "Are there any naughty children here?"
They listen for the names of the children and then write the names in a small book.
Each house then gives the namahage a rice cake as a gift.

__Naughty__ children don't listen to their parents.

C Complete the questions about the festival. Use the prepositions in the box.

for	in	on	to

1. What city is the festival _____?
2. What month is it _____?
3. What kind of costume do the men put _____?
4. Which houses do the namahage go _____?

5. Who are they looking _____?
6. What do they listen _____?
7. What do they write _____?

D Cover **B**. Ask and answer the questions in **C** with a partner.

Men dress up as *namahage* in Oga City, Japan.

Getting outdoors is one way to spend your staycation.

ACTIVE ENGLISH Try it out!

A Look at the word below and answer the questions. Work with a partner.

staycation

1. "Staycation" is a new word in English. It's a combination of two words. What two other words does it look like?

2. What do you think it means? Write a definition here.

_____

B Read about staycations. Rewrite your definition in **A**. Why do you think people take staycations?

- "Staycation" is a combination of two words: *stay + vacation*
- When you take a staycation, you **stay** in your hometown and take a short **vacation** (from 1–2 days to a week). You take a break from your daily routine.
- A staycation is a chance to visit a new local place or try a new activity.

C Work with a partner. Answer the questions. Plan your own weekend staycation.

1. How are you preparing for your staycation?
2. During your staycation, who are you spending time with?
3. What new place are you going to?
4. What place are you relaxing at?

Staycation activities
relax at a park or spa
eat at a nice restaurant
go to a new place
take a class
organize your home
your idea: _____

D Join another pair. Ask and answer questions about your staycations.

" How are you preparing for your staycation?

I'm turning off my phone! "

8A GOALS Now I can . . .

Talk about important dates ____

Say I know or don't know something ____

1. Yes, I can.
2. Mostly, yes.
3. Not yet.

110 | UNIT 8

VOCABULARY

A Read about the Highland Games. Look up any words you don't know. Then ask and answer the questions with a partner.

The Highland Games **take place** in Scotland **every year** in the spring, summer, and fall.

Many things happen at the **festival**:

- People wear **traditional** clothes and play traditional sports. One popular **event** is the hammer throw.
- There are bagpipe **parades**.

- People from around the world **perform** traditional Scottish dances. They **compete** to be the best.

Thousands of people **attend** the games. People also **celebrate** the games in countries like Brazil and New Zealand.

Don't miss the festival, and take lots of photos!

1. Where are the games? _____
2. How often do they take place? _____
3. When do they take place? _____
4. How many people attend? _____
5. What happens at the games? _____
6. Is this event interesting to you? Why or why not? _____

B Think of another sporting event or sports festival. Tell a partner about it. Use the questions in **A**.

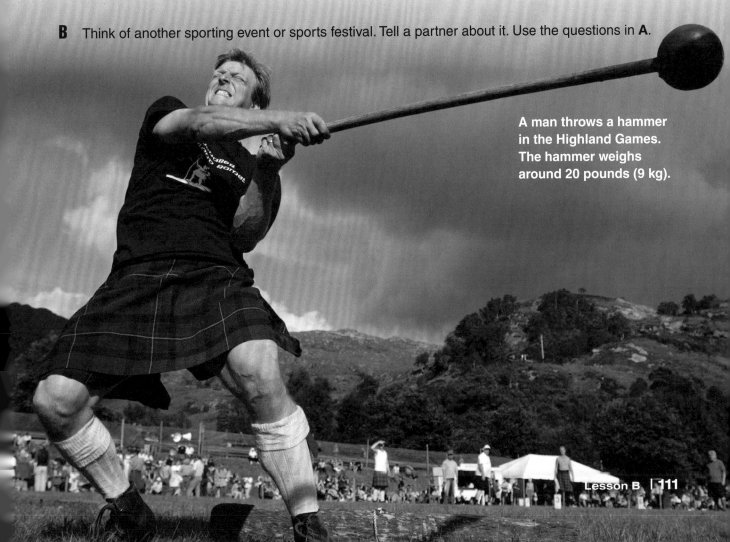

A man throws a hammer in the Highland Games. The hammer weighs around 20 pounds (9 kg).

BURNING MAN:
ART IN THE
DESERT

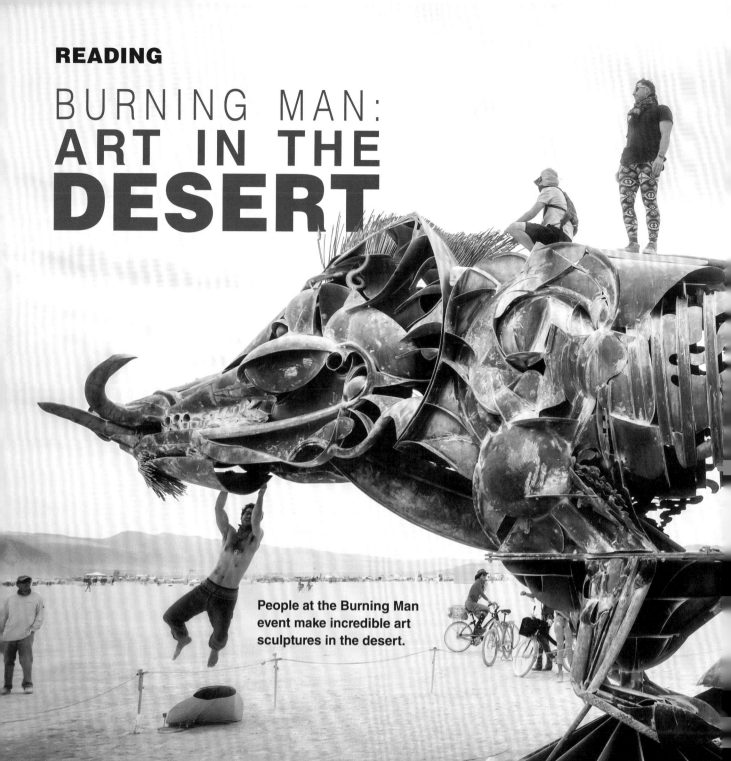

People at the Burning Man event make incredible art sculptures in the desert.

A Look at the photo and read the caption. Who are the people in the photo? What are they doing?

B Read the first paragraph. Answer the questions.

   1. What is Black Rock City?

   2. Why do people go there?

C Read the article. What things do people do at Burning Man? Check (✓) the correct answers.

☐ build something

☐ buy their favorite art

☐ cook

☐ dance

☐ drive cars

☐ leave their garbage behind

☐ make art

☐ watch performances

Every year in late August, more than 75,000 people travel to the desert[1] for the Burning[2] Man event. This event takes place over nine days. At the event, people make a "city" there and call it Black Rock City. There are streets but no cars in Black Rock City. People walk around or ride bicycles, but they don't go fast. The speed limit is only 5 mph (8 kph). Most of the people stay in tents. People live simply. They cook together, dance, perform, and make art. The performances are free, and it doesn't cost anything to look at the art.

It is very hot during the day—sometimes over 100° F (38° C). Most of the performances take place at night. Burning Man Information Radio is on 24 hours a day. It gives general information about performances, art locations, and other news.

During the week, people build a large wooden man in the city. At the end of the week, they burn the man. Then everyone cleans up their area. There is one rule: everything you bring to the desert, you have to take home with you.

Everyone leaves the desert. There is no more Black Rock City, until next August. 🎧69

[1] A **desert** area has little water and not many plants.
[2] A **burning** object is on fire.

D **Explain.** Why are these things mentioned in the article? Use each one in a sentence.

1. bicycles _People use bicycles, not cars, in Black Rock City._

2. the desert _____

3. a radio station _____

4. tents _____

5. a wooden man _____

E Do you want to go to the Burning Man event? Why or why not?

Balloons come in many shapes and colors.

LISTENING

A Look at the photo and the caption. Answer the questions.

1. What do you see in the photo?

2. What do you think is happening?

B Read the sentences. Then listen and learn about the International Balloon Fiesta. Circle *True* or *False*. Then rewrite the false sentences to make them true. 🎧 70

> **i** *Fiesta* is the Spanish word for "party."

1. The Balloon Fiesta is in the summer.   True   False

   _____

2. The balloons come only from the US.   True   False

   _____

3. The balloon race is in the afternoon.   True   False

   _____

4. Some visitors join teams.   True   False

   _____

C **Listen for numbers.** Listen again. Match the numbers to the things they describe. 🎧 70

9	balloons in interesting shapes
100	days
550	different countries
22	teams from around the world
8	traditional balloons

> **Pronunciation**
> 550 = five hundred (and) fifty

D Imagine you are at the Balloon Fiesta. Do you want to help with the balloons or just watch? Tell a partner.

114 | **UNIT 8**

GRAMMAR

A Read the Unit 8, Lesson B Grammar Reference in the appendix. Complete the exercises. Then do the exercises below.

QUESTIONS WITH *WHEN* AND *HOW LONG*	
When is the balloon fiesta? **How long** is the balloon fiesta? 　　It's **from** October 5 **to** October 13.* **When** is summer break? **How long** is summer break? 　　It's **from** July **to** September.	Use *from . . . to* to answer questions (about dates and seasons) with *when* and *how long*.
When is the balloon fiesta? 　　It's **in** October. / It's **in** the fall. 　　It's **in** the early evening. / It's **in** 2021.	*In* is used to show <u>a point in time</u>. Use *in* before months, seasons, times of day, and years.
How long is the balloon fiesta? 　　It lasts **for** nine days. 　　Nine days.	*For* is used to show a <u>period of time</u>.
Remember: When you read it aloud, say "October fifth to October thirteenth."	

B Complete the conversation with *When*, *How long*, or a preposition. Then practice in pairs.

A: _____ does your vacation start?

B: _____ Friday.

A: _____ is your break?

B: It lasts _____ two weeks, _____ July 16 _____ July 30.

A: Do you have any plans?

B: Yeah. I'm going to California. I'm attending Comic-Con. It takes place every year _____ July.

A: Cool! _____ do you leave?

B: _____ July 21. My flight is _____ the afternoon.

A: _____ are you away?

B: I'm there _____ a week. I return home _____ July 28.

A: Sounds good. So, _____ is the flight from Lima to San Diego?

B: Nine hours!

> **ℹ Using *on***
> Use *on* with dates and days of the week.
> *on Monday / on March 7*

C Work with a partner. Make a new conversation about your vacation. Use the conversation in **B** as a model.

D Say your conversation for another pair. When you listen to the other pair, answer the questions.

1. How long is the speaker's break?
2. Where is he or she going?
3. When does he or she leave?
4. How long is he or she staying at the event?

Every year, more than 130,000 comic book fans attend Comic-Con International in San Diego, California. At the event, they learn about new comic books and sci-fi movies and TV shows.

The Fringe Festival takes place every summer in Edinburgh, Scotland.

ACTIVE ENGLISH Try it out!

A Read about the Edinburgh Fringe Festival. Then, with a partner, write down some questions about it.

WHAT: The Fringe Festival WHERE: Edinburgh, Scotland WHEN: Three weeks in August NEXT ONE: August 6–30	The Fringe Festival is the largest arts celebration in the world. People watch dance, music, and comedy performances—and more! Some of the performers are famous, but many are not. The shows are for both children and adults. It's a lot of fun!

Student A: Use the words to write three questions about the Fringe Festival.

1. where / take place _____

2. how long _____

3. what kind / performances _____

Student B: Use the words to write three questions about the Fringe Festival.

1. what month _____

2. what kind / festival _____

3. who / shows for _____

B Take turns asking and answering the questions in **A** with your partner.

C Think of a festival. Choose two words from the box to describe it. Ask your partner about his or her festival. Can you guess it?

Examples: a traditional arts festival, a summer film festival, a new music festival

A: What kind of festival is it?

B: It's a traditional arts festival.

A: When does it take place?

| **Different types of festivals** |
| arts, cultural, film, music, summer*, new, traditional *or any other season |

D **WRITING** Write about your festival. Use the text in **A** as a model.

8B GOALS Now I can . . .

State when and how long an event is _____

Describe what happens at a festival _____

1. Yes, I can.
2. Mostly, yes.
3. Not yet.

GLOBAL VOICES

A Study the words in the Word Bank. Then read the information below.

In this video, two people (JY and Lara) are talking about holidays. JY talks about a **lunar calendar**. A lunar calendar uses the moon to measure time. It is a very old calendar. Do you know about it?

B Watch the first part of the video. Circle the correct answers.

1. JY is from **Korea** / **Japan**. Lara is from **Italy** / **Spain**.

2. JY is talking about a **new** / **traditional** holiday. The date for this holiday **changes** / **doesn't change** every year.

C Watch JY talk about a holiday. Complete the sentences on the left.

JY

1. She is talking about a _____ year's celebration.

2. This year it's on January _____. Next year it's on February _____.

3. The family gathers at _____ house.

4. Everyone eats rice cake _____.

Lara

1. She is talking about *semana santa*, holy _____.

2. You celebrate it around Easter (in _____ or _____).

3. The family gathers at _____ house.

4. Everyone eats a kind of French _____.

5. There are _____ and costumes.

D Now watch Lara talk about another holiday. Complete the sentences on the right.

E Think of a holiday you know. Answer the questions in the chart. Then tell your partner about it.

What is the name of the holiday?	
When is it?	
Where do people gather for the holiday?	
What do they eat?	

Colorful lights at a Korean new year's celebration

TOGETHER

9

LOOK AT THE PHOTO. ANSWER THE QUESTIONS.

1. What are the women doing?

2. How do you think they know each other?

WARM-UP VIDEO

A In the places below, when do people usually move out* of their parents' homes? Guess with a partner.

Place	Age		
the United States	19	23	26 or older
many Latin American countries	19	23	26 or older
some European countries	19	23	26 or older

*When you **move out**, you leave a house and go to live in another place.

B Watch the video. Circle the correct ages in **A**.

C Watch the video again. Circle **T** for *true* or **F** for *false*. Correct the false sentences.

1. In the US, college students usually live alone.   **T   F**

2. After college, many students in the US move back in with their parents.   **T   F**

3. In Latin America, many college students live with their parents.   **T   F**

4. In Europe, most college students live with roommates.   **T   F**

5. Many big cities are expensive, so some people need roommates.   **T   F**

D Talk about your country. When do people leave their parents' homes? Do they live with someone else?

Visitors in the
Starry Art Museum
in Shanghai, China

GOALS

Lesson A
/ Explain how often you do things
/ Make and respond to apologies

Lesson B
/ Talk about friendship
/ Ask questions about friends

VOCABULARY

A Say the chores in the Word Bank with your teacher. Talk about their meanings. Then tell a partner what chores you do at home.

" | After dinner, I do the dishes.

B Read the tips below.

1. Tell a partner what it is about.

2. Then do the following:

- Complete ❶–❸ with verbs from the Word Bank.

- Complete ❹ with *do* or *make*. Check your answers at the bottom of the page.

WORD BANK

chores
    clean (a room)
    do the dishes
    do the laundry
    make breakfast / dinner
    make your bed
    take out the garbage

Many expressions in English use *do* and *make*. How many are in the tips? Circle them. Do you know any others?

Life with Roommates
Tips for Living Together

❶ **Make a list** of **chores**. Decide when to . . .

- _____ **the dishes**.
- ____*clean*____ **common areas*** (like the bathroom).
- _____ **the garbage**.

❷ Keep your own room tidy: _____ **your bed** and _____ **your laundry**.

❸ _____ **dinner** and eat together sometimes.

❹ Don't _____ **noise** when people are trying to _____ **homework** or sleep.

*In a house, a **common area** is a room everyone uses.

C Take turns reading ❶–❹ aloud with a partner.

1. Do you think these are good ideas? Why or why not?

2. Add one more idea to the list. Then tell the class.

4. make noise, do homework

LISTENING

A **Activate knowledge.** Look at the photo and read the caption. In your opinion, is it good to live with roommates? Why or why not? Tell a partner.

WORD BANK

loud = making a lot of noise

pay the rent = give money to live in a house

B **Predict.** Read the outline. Try to guess the answers with a partner.

LIVING WITH A ROOMMATE

The good things

1. You save _____.
   a. You each pay part of the rent.
   b. You can go shopping together, too.
2. You share the _____.
   a. You do _____ and your roommate _____ the garbage.
3. It's _____ to have a roommate.
   a. You aren't _____. A roommate is like a friend.

The problems

4. You and your roommate are different.
   a. You _____ often, but your roommate doesn't.
5. Sometimes _____ is a problem.
   a. Your roommate listens to loud _____ when you are studying or sleeping.

C Listen for the good things. Complete items 1, 2, and 3 in **B**. Write a word or phrase. 71

D Listen for the problems. Complete items 4 and 5. 72

E Answer the questions with a partner.

1. Think about your answer in **A**. Is it still the same?
2. Look at the problems in **B**. When these bad things happen, what can roommates do?

In expensive cities (like Paris), students and other young people sometimes live with roommates.

SPEAKING

Are they good roommates?

A The men in the photo are roommates. What are they doing? Tell a partner.

B Read and listen to the conversation between another group of roommates. Then answer the questions. 🎧73

Emilio: Hey, guys.

Adam: Hey, Emilio. What's up? Do you want to join us?

Emilio: Thanks, but not tonight. Actually, I'm trying to sleep and the game is a little loud.

Adam: Oh, sorry about that!

Emilio: No problem. I don't usually go to bed this early, but I have a big test in the morning.

Adam: We'll be quiet.

Emilio: Great. Thanks.

Adam: Sure. Good luck with the test tomorrow.

1. Adam apologizes (says he is sorry) to Emilio. Why? Underline his apology.

2. How does Emilio respond to the apology?

C Practice the conversation with a partner.

D Choose a situation and role-play it. Use the conversation in **B** and the expressions in the Speaking Strategy to help you.

Situation 1

Student A: You want to do your laundry, but your roommate's clothes are in the washing machine.

Student B: You forgot about your clothes. You'll get them now.

Situation 2

Student A: Your parents plan to visit this afternoon. A lot of your roommate's dishes are in the sink, and the house is very messy.

Student B: It's your turn to clean today. You'll do it now.

E Perform your role play for another pair. Don't read your conversation.

F Repeat **D** and **E**. Switch roles and do the other situation.

> **SPEAKING STRATEGY** 🎧74
> **Apologizing**
>
> | **Making an apology** |
> | --- |
> | (I'm) sorry. |
> | (I'm) sorry about that. |
> | I'm really sorry. [stronger] |
> | **Responding to an apology** |
> | No problem. |
> | That's OK / all right. |
> | Don't worry about it. |

GRAMMAR

A Read about Emilio. Then circle the correct word in sentences 1–3.

Emilio <u>is</u> **never** late.

Emilio **always** <u>pays</u> his rent on time.

Emilio <u>doesn't</u> **usually** <u>go</u> to bed early.

Frequency Adverbs	
always	100%
usually	
often	
sometimes	
hardly ever	
never	0%

1. Frequency adverbs come **before** / **after** the verb *be*.
2. Most frequency adverbs come **before** / **after** other main verbs.
3. Most frequency adverbs come **before** / **after** *not*.

B Read the Unit 9, Lesson A Grammar Reference in the appendix.
Complete the exercises. Then do the exercises below.

C **PRONUNCIATION: Frequency adverbs** Listen and write the adverbs in 1–3. Then say the
sentences with a partner. 🎧75

1. My roommate is _____ home. He's _____ working.

2. We _____ do the chores together.

3. _____ we play video games. My roommate _____ wins.

D Linda and Amy are roommates. They're having problems these days. In your notebook, write each
sentence with the frequency adverb given.

Linda says:	Amy says:
1. Amy takes out the trash. (hardly ever)	1. Linda is watching TV in the main room. I can't do my homework there. (always)
2. Her dirty dishes are in the sink. (always)	2. She leaves her clothes in the washing machine. (usually)
3. She makes noise at night. (often)	3. She's quiet in the morning. (never)
4. She doesn't pay her rent on time. (sometimes)	4. She goes out, but she doesn't lock the front door. (sometimes)

E Work with a partner. Use the sentences in **D**. One person is Linda;
the other is Amy. Talk about your problems. Can you make
things better?

❝ Amy, you hardly ever take out the trash, and your dirty dishes are . . .

I'm sorry about that, Linda. I'm busy studying for exams. ❞

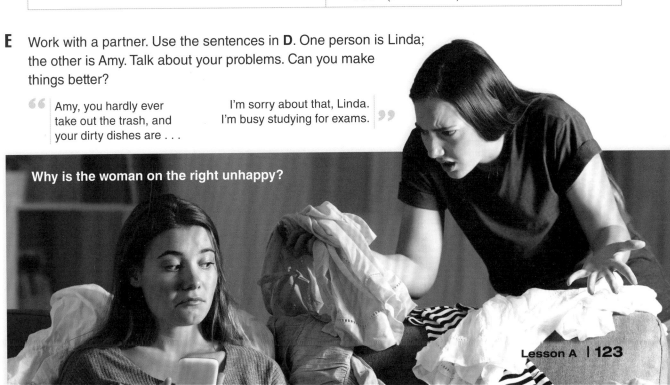

Why is the woman on the right unhappy?

ACTIVE ENGLISH Try it out!

A Imagine you are looking for a roommate to share your apartment. Read the questions below. In your answers, use frequency adverbs.

ROOMMATE QUESTIONNAIRE				
QUESTIONS	My answer	Partner 1:	Partner 2:	Partner 3:
1. Do you clean your room often? How about common areas?				
2. After you cook, do you do the dishes?				
3. Do you study in your own room?				
4. When do you wake up? When do you go to bed?				
5. What do you do on the weekend? Do you ever have parties?				
6. Do you have a job? Do you pay rent on time?				
7. You forgot to take out the trash. What do you say to your roommate?				
8. Your question:				

B Use the questions in **A** to interview three classmates.

" Do you clean your room often?

Yeah, I usually clean my room and make my bed every day. I also clean the apartment once a week. How about you? "

C Think about your three interviews. Who is the best roommate for you? Why? Tell a partner.

" Maria is the best roommate for me. We're very similar. For example, . . .

9A GOALS   Now I can . . .

Explain how often I do things _____

Make and respond to apologies _____

1. Yes, I can.
2. Mostly, yes.
3. Not yet.

VOCABULARY

A Read the information about teenagers in the US, paying special attention to the words in blue. How do you think they feel about friendship? Circle a number to complete the sentences.

Friendship in the US

51% of teenagers say they **get along** well with others. What else do they say about **friendship**? Read below to find out!

Number of close friends

20% / 98% say they have one or more **close friends**. **20% / 98%** say they have six or more.

Good friends: Close or far away?

35% / 87% say they have a **good friend** at school. **35% / 87%** have a good friend who lives far away.

Meeting friends online or in person

- 15% of teens **make friends** with new people online.
- Friends like to **keep in touch** online. **24% / 60%** say they spend time with their friends online every day.
- Friends **hang out** in person, too. **24% / 60%** say they meet their friends in person every day.

B Check your answers on page 217. Are any of the answers surprising? Discuss with a partner.

C What about you? Check (✓) the statements that are true for you. Share your answers with a partner.

☐ I have three or more close friends.

☐ I have a good friend at school.

☐ I keep in touch with my friends online.

☐ I like to hang out with my friends in person more than online.

☐ I meet my friends in person every day.

Friends hang out at a skate park.

THE WONDERFUL GIFT OF FRIENDSHIP

We all need friends. Friendships start and sometimes they change. How does that happen? Let's take a closer look.

How do friendships start?

Many important friendships start when we're young. Sometimes we're children. Other times, we're in high school or college. Two people meet and become best friends. The friendship lasts a long time.

Very often, it's easy to make new friends when we're younger. There are some reasons for this. For one, we often make new friends at work or at school, or we live in the same neighborhood as our friends. We spend a lot of time near[1] each other, and it's easy to get together[2].

Also, we have more free time when we're young. We have many chances to hang out with our

Sometimes we make friends at work. These park rangers work in Yosemite National Park.

friends and have fun. When we do activities together, we become close friends.

How do friendships change?

When we're older, some friendships change. How does this happen? We now have a job. Some of us have a family. Our lives are very busy. We don't have a lot of time to hang out with friends.

Also, some of us move away from our friends. We don't live near our friends anymore, and it's hard to keep in touch. We don't do things together, and over time, this changes the friendship.

And finally, we change as we get older. Our personalities[3] are different. We want to do different things. We spend time with different—and new—friends. 🎧76

[1]*If you live **near** something, you live close to it.*
[2]*When you **get together** with someone, you meet up with them.*
[3]*A person's **personality** is how they are.*

A Look at the photo and read the caption. Then answer the question below. Check (✓) your answer and share it with a partner.

What is the best age for making friends?

☐ as a child

☐ as a teenager

☐ in your twenties

☐ in your thirties or older

B **Use headings to predict.** Read the questions in bold in the article. Think of one or more answers to each question. Tell a partner.

C Read the article. Are any of your ideas from **B** mentioned? If yes, underline them.

D Read the article again. Which reason is *not* mentioned in the article? Cross out one answer to each question.

1. How do friendships start?

   a. Two people meet each other online.

   b. People meet at work or at school.

   c. People live near each other and spend time together.

2. How do friendships change?

   a. Friends don't live near each other and it's hard to meet.

   b. Friends have a big fight and stop talking to each other.

   c. Friends are busy and don't have time to meet.

E Which things in **D** sometimes happen to you and your friends? Tell a partner.

F Tell a partner about one of your friends in as much detail as you can.

❝ My friend Cam and I are busy, but we still hang out a lot together. We're on the same soccer team.

Finding Fukue (foo-koo-ay) is a short film about two childhood friends, Fukue and Jessica.

LISTENING

A Do you remember your friends from childhood? Are you still friends with any of them?

B Listen to the first part of a story about Jessica Stuart and her friend. Complete the sentences. 77

1. Jessica is _____ years old. She's from _____. Her family goes to Japan. She goes to school there.

2. Fukue is a _____, too. She goes to the same school. She _____ Jessica.

3. They meet at _____. They start a friendship.

C **Listen and sequence.** Read the sentences. Listen. What happens in the story? Number the parts from 1–7. 78

a. Jessica goes to Japan to find Fukue. _____

b. Jessica and Fukue hang out together. _____

c. Jessica's family moves to Japan. __1__

d. Jessica's family returns to Canada. _____

e. Jessica meets Fukue. _____

f. Jessica finds Fukue. _____

g. Jessica and Fukue don't keep in touch. _____

D Listen again. Circle **T** for *true* or **F** for *false*. 78

1. The girls are in elementary school.	T	F
2. Jessica learns English from Fukue.	T	F
3. Jessica is a musician.	T	F
4. First, Jessica finds Fukue's brother.	T	F
5. Jessica remembers Fukue, but Fukue doesn't remember Jessica.	T	F

E Can Fukue and Jessica be friends now? Can they keep in touch easily?

GRAMMAR

A Read the Unit 9, Lesson B Grammar Reference in the appendix. Complete the exercises. Then do the exercises below.

REVIEW OF QUESTION FORMS: *BE*				ANSWERS
Wh- word	*be*	Noun / Pronoun		
Who	's / is	Jessica?		She's Fukue's friend.
Where	's / is	Fukue?		She's in Japan.
	Are	they	old friends?	Yes, they are. *No, they aren't. / No, they're not.*

REVIEW OF QUESTION FORMS: OTHER VERBS					ANSWERS
Wh- word	*do*	Noun / Pronoun	Verb		
When	do	you	hang out	with friends?	After school.
How long	does	she	study?		For about an hour.
	Do	you	make	friends easily?	Yes, I do. / *No, I don't.*

B Read each question and answer. Circle the letter of the incorrect part.

1. Is she your friend?   No, she not.
   A   B   C   D

2. Are you and Jon good friends?   Yes, they are.
   A   B   C   D

3. Is Paolo have a lot of friends?   Yes, he does.
   A   B   C   D

4. Does Amy goes to school every day?   Yes, she does.
   A   B   C D

C Use the words in the box to complete the questions. You will use some words more than once.

are	do	how	is	what	when	where

1. ____When____ ____do____ you meet your friends?
2. _____ you a good listener?
3. _____ many friends _____ you have?
4. _____ _____ you go with your friends?
5. _____ you keep in touch with your old friends?
6. _____ _____ you usually do with your friends?
7. _____ your friends the same age as you?
8. _____ _____ a good place to meet new friends?
9. _____ you have a best friend?
10. _____ _____ you keep in touch with your friends?

D Ask and answer the questions in **C** with a partner.

Two good friends meet at their favorite cafe.

ACTIVE ENGLISH Try it out!

A Read the sentence about friendship. Do you agree with it? Discuss with a partner.

A good friend is hard to find.

B Unscramble the words to make questions.

1. are / sentences / what / about / these _____

2. mean / does / sentence / this / what _____

3. with / ideas / you / these / do / agree _____

4. which / favorite / is / one / your _____

C Work with a partner. Take turns asking and answering the questions in **B** about these sentences.

1. It's hard to keep in touch with old friends.

2. Good friends are good listeners.

3. Your friends are the same as your family.

4. Be slow to start and slow to end a friendship.

D **WRITING** Choose an idea from **C**. Copy the sentence and write about your own experience.

It's hard to keep in touch with old friends. I know Mia from junior high school. We're the same age. Sometimes we text, but I don't see her anymore. She lives far away. I miss her.*

*I miss her means I feel sad because I can't see her anymore.

9B GOALS Now I can . . .

Talk about friendship _____

Ask questions about friends _____

1. Yes, I can.
2. Mostly, yes.
3. Not yet.

GLOBAL VOICES

A Read about Jackson and David. Then complete the sentences with the words in the box.

WORD BANK
friend ⟷ enemy

classmates	close	fight	same	spend

1. Jackson and David are _____.
2. They're friends, but not _____ friends.
3. They _____ time together sometimes.
4. They _____ sometimes, too.
5. They're "frenemies": both friends and enemies at the _____ time.

B Watch the video. Complete the questions.

1. _____ do you like him?
2. _____ do you usually do with your friends?
3. _____ you sometimes fight with your friends?
4. _____ you have any "frenemies"?
   ___Why___ are you friends with these people?
5. _____ often do you talk to your friends?
6. _____ it easy for you to make friends?

C Read the sentences about Alex. Watch the video again. Circle the correct words.

1. Mike is his **old** / **new** friend.
2. They both like **movies** / **sports** and dancing.
3. Alex hangs out with his friends, and they **talk** / **go out**.
4. They also play **soccer** / **basketball** together.
5. Alex **has** / **doesn't have** frenemies.
6. He **video chats** / **doesn't video chat** with his friends.
7. He says it's **easy** / **hard** to make good friends.
8. He meets new people at work and at **parties** / **school**.

D Reread the sentences in **C**. Complete the task.

1. Make the sentences in **C** about yourself.

   he / *his* → *I* / *my*   *they* → *we*
   Alex → *I*   *Mike* → your friend's name

   ❝ I hang out with my friends, and we talk. Alex and I are similar.

2. Are you the same as Alex? Tell a partner.

Are these two men friends or "frenemies"?

REAL WORLD LINK AN OUTDOOR FESTIVAL

At this summer music festival in California, US, a 36-foot-tall (almost 11 meters) astronaut moves across the grounds.

A Answer the questions. Then share your answers with a partner.

1. How often do you attend festivals?

☐ often ☐ hardly ever

☐ sometimes ☐ never

2. What kind of festivals or outdoor* events do you go to?

B Read the information about a festival. Guess the missing words. Then listen and write the missing words. What do you think of the festival? 🎧79

SUMMER FESTIVAL: OUTDOORS IN THE CITY!

Do you live and work in the city? Do you also like to spend time outdoors? Well, we have an exciting festival for you!

- For 10 days in _____, our outdoor festival has many free _____ at different places around the city.

- Many people attend the festival with their friends and family. Other people come alone and make new _____. Everyone gets along at the festival!

- Our festival is _____ very popular, so get your tickets online soon!

---

*outdoor = not inside

C Unscramble the questions. Then, with a partner, ask and answer the questions about the festival in **B**.

Student A: Ask questions 1, 3, 5, and 7.

Student B: Ask questions 2, 4, 6, and 8.

1. season / in / what / it / does / happen

   _____

2. who / the / is / festival / for

   _____

3. festival / how / is / long / the

   _____

4. take / does / in / it / what / place / month

   _____

5. it / anything / cost / to attend / does

   _____

6. the / place / events / one / are / in

   _____

7. with / do / people / go / who / usually

   _____

8. a / event / it / friendly / is

   _____

D Read about the outdoor event ideas. Rank them from 1 (most fun) to 6 (least fun). Share your ideas with a partner.

Event ideas

_____ Rooftop yoga class: *Practice yoga with beautiful city views.*

_____ Beach cleanup: *Pick up garbage on the beach.*

_____ Learn to read a map: *Prepare for your next trip.*

_____ Go to a concert: *Listen to great music under the stars.*

_____ See a movie: *Go for a picnic and stay for an outdoor movie.*

_____ Go for a nighttime run in the park: *Use a headlamp to see.*

E You are planning your own summer outdoor festival. Think of three fun events. Choose ideas from **D** or use your own ideas. In your notebook, write this information about your three events: event name, location, day, and time.

F Work with a partner. Complete the task and then switch roles.

Student A: Tell your partner about your three events in **E**.

Student B: Listen. Then ask a follow-up question about each event.

i Follow-up questions

How long is the event?
Do I need to bring anything?
It's my first time. Is that OK?

G **You Choose** Choose an option to tell others about your event(s).

Option 1: Make a chart with the schedule for your three events. Present the information to a partner. Talk about each event.

Option 2: Choose one of your events. Write a social media post about it. Give the basic information and one or two interesting details.

Option 3: Choose one of your events. Write a script and record a radio ad for the event.

" My first event is a movie night at Baker Park. It's on Saturday at 8:45.

It sounds fun. How much does it cost? "

H Read about or listen to your partner's event(s). Do you want to attend? Why or why not?

HOME

LOOK AT THE PHOTO. ANSWER THE QUESTIONS.

1. Do you like this apartment building? Why or why not?

2. Look in the windows. What things do you see in the rooms? Check (✓) your answers.

☐ bed   ☐ people

☐ chairs   ☐ table

☐ door   ☐ window

☐ kitchen   ☐ curtains

WARM-UP VIDEO

A In your house, are the rooms big or small? Tell a partner.

B Watch the video with the sound off. Check (✓) the three things people are doing in each room.

Room 1

☐ cooking   ☐ reading

☐ playing   ☐ sleeping

Room 2

☐ cooking   ☐ reading

☐ eating and drinking   ☐ watching TV

Room 3

☐ eating   ☐ studying

☐ sleeping   ☐ watching TV

C Watch the video again. Which rooms in **B** do you like? Why? Tell a partner.

" I like Room 2.
It has a big TV.

I don't like Room 2.
It's too small. I like Room 3. "

This colorful apartment building was built in northern Sweden in 2013.

GOALS

Lesson A
/ Identify objects and rooms in a home
/ Show surprise

Lesson B
/ Describe rooms in a house
/ Talk about ways to improve a room or house

VOCABULARY

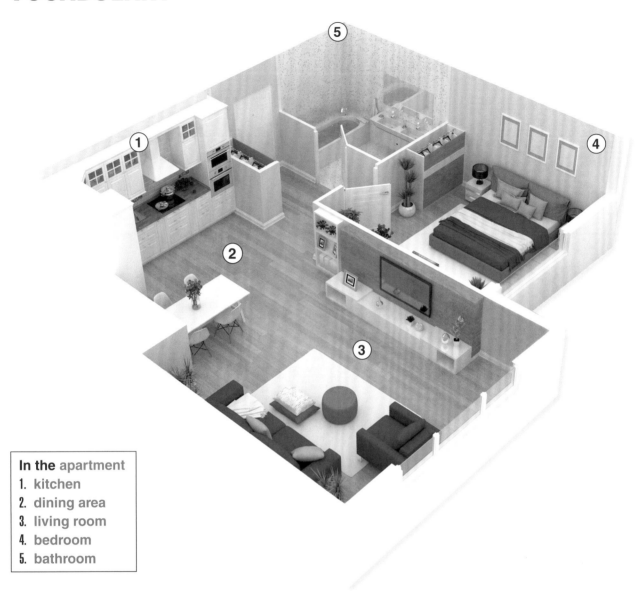

In the apartment
1. kitchen
2. dining area
3. living room
4. bedroom
5. bathroom

A Look at the apartment. Say words 1–5 with your teacher.

B Practice with a partner. Point to a place in the apartment and say it.
Take turns. Then cover words 1–5 and practice again.

    " This is the kitchen.

C Say the words in the Word Bank. Watch your teacher point to the things in
the picture.

WORD BANK
bed
closet
shower with bathtub
sofa
table with four chairs

D With a partner, make sentences. Point to the things in the picture.

There's a _____ in the _____.

room / area

E Look at the apartment again. Is your home similar or different?

    " My home is different.
It has two bedrooms.

LISTENING

A **Build background knowledge.** Read the sentences in the Word Bank. Then look at the photo. Answer the questions.

1. Do you live in an apartment building? If yes, on what floor?
2. Where is the Copan Building? Is it big or small? How many people live there?

WORD BANK
I **live in** an apartment / house.
I **live on** the third **floor**.
A store is on the **ground** (1ˢᵗ) **floor**.

B Listen to a speaker talk about the Copan Building. Write a number. 🎧80

1. The year it opened: _____
2. Number of floors: _____
3. Number of elevators: _____
4. Number of apartments: _____

C The speaker talks about an apartment in the building. 🎧81

WORD BANK
elevator

1. Read items 1–8.
2. Then listen. Choose the correct answers.

The apartment has _____.

☐ **1.** a view
☐ **2.** two bedrooms
☐ **3.** two beds
☐ **4.** a big living area
☐ **5.** a kitchen area
☐ **6.** a big closet
☐ **7.** a bathroom with a large shower
☐ **8.** a washing machine

D Listen again. Choose **T** for *true* or **F** for *false*. Correct the false sentences. 🎧81

1. The apartment is on the third floor. T F
2. You do laundry on the second floor. T F
3. There are over 70 businesses on the ground floor. T F
4. A gym and art gallery are in the building. T F
5. You can walk to the subway in 15 minutes. T F

E Discuss the questions with a partner.

1. Is the apartment a good place to live? Why or why not?
2. Are there apartment buildings like the Copan in your city?

❝ My city is small. We live in houses, not apartments.

Five thousand (5,000) people live in the Copan Building in São Paulo, Brazil. The building is so large it has its own zip code.

SPEAKING

A Read and listen to the conversation. Then answer the questions. 🎧82

1. What things are good about Jun's new apartment?

2. What's the problem with it?

WORD BANK
rent
stairs
up ⟷ down

Colorful staircases in Bugis Village, Singapore

Max: So, Jun, how's your new place?

Jun: Great. Look, I've got some photos on my phone.

Max: Nice. It's big.

Jun: Yeah, and the rent is cheap.

Max: Really? That's great.

Jun: Yeah, I like it. There's just one problem.

Max: What's that?

Jun: There's no elevator and I'm on the fifth floor.

Max: No way. So you walk up and down the stairs every day?

Jun: Yeah. It's not easy!

B **PRONUNCIATION: Showing surprise**
Listen once to the sentences. Then listen again and say Max's part. 🎧83

Jun: It's a big place and the rent is cheap.

Max: Really? (↗) That's great.

Jun: There's no elevator and I'm on the fifth floor.

Max: No way. (↘)

SPEAKING STRATEGY 🎧84
Showing Surprise

Said with rising intonation (↗)	Said with falling intonation (↘)
Really?	You're kidding.
Are you serious?	No way.

C Practice the conversation in **A** with a partner. Then practice again with different expressions.

D Make a new conversation. Talk about two good things and one bad thing. Use the Speaking Strategy and the ideas below. Then act out your conversation for another pair.

Good things about your apartment

It has two bedrooms.

It has a nice view.

You can walk to school.

My idea: _____

Bad things about your apartment

There's no AC and it's 40 degrees.

There's no kitchen.

Your roommate likes loud music.

My idea: _____

WORD BANK
AC = air conditioning

GRAMMAR

A Read the Unit 10, Lesson A Grammar Reference in the appendix. Complete the exercises. Then do the exercises below.

THERE IS / THERE ARE				
Singular	There is / There's	an / *no*	elevator	in the building.
Plural	There are	(two) / *no*	elevators	

Questions			Short Answers
Is there	an elevator	in the building?	Yes, **there is**. / No, *there isn't*.
Are there (any)	elevators		Yes, **there are**. / No, *there aren't*.
How many	elevators	are in the building?	**There's** one. / **There are** two.

B Work with a partner. **Student A:** Turn to page 215. Read the directions there. **Student B:** Your partner is looking for student housing. Follow these steps:

1. Tell your partner about the apartment below.

2. Answer your partner's questions about the apartment's "extras." Use *there is / there are*.

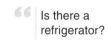

> **❝** Is there a refrigerator?
>
> Yes, there . . .
> It's . . . **❞**

WORD BANK
microwave (oven)
refrigerator
window

About the apartment for rent	Extras (✓ = yes ✗ = no)
It's on the fifth floor. There's one large room. There's no kitchen, but there is a microwave to cook simple food. There's also a small bathroom.	✓ refrigerator (small) ✓ closets (two) ✓ laundry room (on the ground floor) ✗ elevator (stairs only)

C Change roles.

1. Listen to your partner tell you about an apartment. Take notes below.

2. Ask your partner questions to learn about the apartment's extras. Put a ✓ or an ✗.

About the apartment	Extras (✓ = yes ✗ = no)
It's on the . . . _____ _____ _____ _____	_____ washing machine in the apartment? _____ windows in the apartment? _____ closets? _____ bathtub in the bathroom?

D Look at the apartments in **B** and **C**. Do you want to live there? Why or why not?

ACTIVE ENGLISH Try it out!

A Read about the bedroom in the photo. As you read, point to things.

> This is my bedroom. **Next to** the bed (**on the right**), there's a tall lamp. **Near** the lamp, there's a big window. **Across from** the bed (**on the left**), there's a desk and chair. There's a small lamp on the desk. **Above** my bed is my bike. And **in front of** my bed, there's a rug.

B Talk about your room with a partner.

Student A: Think about your bedroom. On a piece of paper, draw your bedroom door and your bed. Then give the paper to your partner. What other things are in your room? Where are they? Tell your partner.

Student B: Listen and draw your partner's bedroom.

C **Student A:** Check your partner's drawing. Does it look like your room?

D Switch roles and do **B** and **C** again. Are your rooms similar or different?

WORD BANK
lamp
rug

10A GOALS Now I can . . .

Identify objects and rooms in a home _____

Show surprise _____

1. Yes, I can.
2. Mostly, yes.
3. Not yet.

VOCABULARY

A Say the colors with your teacher. Then ask a partner: What is your favorite color?

black   dark blue   brown   green   pink   red   white

blue   light blue   gray   orange   purple   bright yellow

B Look at the photo. Answer the questions with a partner.

1. What things are in the room? What colors are they?

2. When you look at the room, how do you feel?

    Complete this sentence with a word from the Word Bank.

    This room makes me feel _____.

3. Do you like the room? Why or why not?

    The colors are very bright. They make me
    feel happy. I like the room.

WORD BANK
Feelings
happy ⟷ unhappy, sad
relaxed ⟷ nervous, uncomfortable

C Find another photo of a room in a house. Answer the questions in **B** about it with a partner.

D Write the name of a color that makes you feel . . .

1. relaxed _____

2. uncomfortable _____

3. happy _____

4. sad _____

This is a very colorful living room.

THE **POWER** OF **COLOR**

What are the best colors for rooms in your home?

We see color everywhere. It makes our world beautiful, but it can also affect[1] our feelings and behavior.[2] For this reason, it is important to use the right colors in different rooms in a home.

For example, use light colors (light blue, green, or gray) in a bedroom or living area. They help us feel relaxed.

Other colors—like red, orange, and yellow—are different. They make us feel alert[3] and sometimes hungry, studies show. For this reason, they can be good to use in a dining area or a kitchen.

A room with some red, orange, or yellow can also feel happy, so these colors can be good in a living area. But these colors are very strong,[4]

and it's best to only use a little of them. People can feel nervous in rooms with too many dark or bright colors.

Other colors help us work or study. Many people think white walls and bright lights are best for this. But people are often uncomfortable in this kind of room. Sometimes in a bright white room, it's too hard to think. Instead, use white with another color, especially light blue. In a home office or a room for studying, light blue and white can help people relax and think better. 🎧85

[1] If something **affects** you, it changes you in some way.
[2] Your **behavior** is the way you act.
[3] If you are **alert**, you feel very awake and ready to do things.
[4] A **strong** color is bright or intense.

Dark red, especially when used with brown or black, can make a room feel warm and comfortable.

A Look at the photo and tell a partner:

1. What things are in the room?

2. In your opinion, is this room comfortable or not? Do you like it?

B **Make predictions.** Read the title of the article and the question below it. Then, with a partner, guess which colors (a–d) are best for each room (1–5) and match them. One color (or set of colors) is extra.

Room	Good colors for the room
1. bedroom	a. red, orange, or yellow
2. living room	b. white only
3. dining room	c. light blue, light green, or light gray
4. kitchen	d. white and light blue
5. home office / study room	

C **Check predictions.** Read the passage. Check your answers in **B**.

D **Scan for information.** Complete the chart with the correct colors and feelings.

Room color(s)	Feeling(s)
light blue, light green, or light gray	1. _____
2. _____ _____	alert, sometimes 3. _____, and happy
lots of dark or bright colors	4. _____
5. _____ walls and _____ lights	uncomfortable
6. light _____ and _____	relaxed and ready to study

E Answer the questions with a partner. Use ideas from the reading.

1. Look at the photo. Is this room good for studying? relaxing? eating? Why? Why not?

2. Talk about a room in your house. What colors are in the room? Is the room good for studying? relaxing? eating? Why? Why not?

LISTENING

A Look at the photo. In your opinion, what are some good and bad things about living in a very small room or home? Tell a partner.

B **Make and check predictions.** Read 1–3 below. With a partner, try to guess the answers. Then listen and write a word in each blank. 86

> ### The problems with a small room
>
> 1. Sometimes, a small room is very _____.
> 2. There's no _____ for all your things. _____ is everywhere.
> 3. The furniture is too big. Then the room feels crowded and _____.

C How can you fix the problems in **B**? Look at the photo again and guess the answers to 1–3. Then listen. Choose the answer(s) for each problem. 87

How to fix* each problem

1. Use ____ in the room.
   a. white or light gray
   b. bright lights
   c. dark colors

2. Put things ____.
   a. in a closet
   b. on shelves
   c. on wall hooks

3. Use ____ in a small room.
   a. a small desk
   b. only one piece of furniture
   c. a folding table

*When you *fix* something, you make it better.

D Work with a partner. Choose a problem in **B**. Explain: how does the idea in **C** fix the problem?

E Discuss the questions with a partner.

1. Can you think of other ideas to add to **C**?
2. Do you do any of these things?

Tiny homes are very small. Many are only about 200 square feet (18.5 square meters).

GRAMMAR

A Read the Unit 10, Lesson B Grammar Reference in the appendix. Complete the exercises. Then do the exercises below.

				VERY AND TOO		
This room	is		**very**	dark.		
He	has	a	**very**	small	apartment.	
The desk	is		**too**	big	for the room.	
It	is		**too**	hard	to study	in a bright room.

B Work with a partner. Follow these steps.

1. Write two sentences about the homes in the photo. Use *too* and *very*, and words from the box.

2. Turn to page 216. Look at the photos there. Repeat step 1.

big	messy
bright	noisy
colorful	old
(un)comfortable	relaxing
crowded	small
dark	your idea:___

Houseboats in Amsterdam, Holland, are cool but they aren't cheap. Also, many are close to the street—and each other—so there isn't a lot of privacy.

C Join another pair. Give them your sentences from **B**. Follow the steps.

1. Read your classmates' sentences. Are any incorrect? If yes, correct them.

2. Do you agree with your classmates' sentences? Tell them.

D Answer the questions with the group.

1. Do you like any of the places in **B**? Why or why not?

2. Think about your home or a family member's. What are good and bad things about it? Use *too* and *very* to explain.

ACTIVE ENGLISH Try it out!

A Look at the photo. With a partner, talk about the problems in this room. How can you fix these problems? On a piece of paper, list and then draw your ideas.

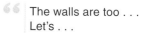
" The walls are too . . .
Let's . . .

B Work with another pair. Explain your ideas to them. When you listen, take notes. What do you like about their ideas?

C Repeat **B** with three other pairs. At the end, review your notes. Then ask a partner: Whose ideas are the best? Why?

D **WRITING** Read about one person's home. Then write about your own.

> I live with my family in an apartment in Santiago. We live on the sixth floor. There are two bedrooms in the apartment. I share one with my sister. In our room, there are two beds, a desk, a bookshelf, and a closet. It's too small for all our clothes! The apartment also has a living room, a dining area, a kitchen, and a very big balcony with lots of plants. I like our apartment a lot!

E Share your writing with a partner. Are your homes similar or different? Give examples.

10B GOALS　　Now I can . . .

Describe rooms in a house _____

Talk about ways to improve a room or house _____

1. Yes, I can.
2. Mostly, yes.
3. Not yet.

GLOBAL VOICES

A Read the information below. Look up the underlined words. Answer the questions.

    1. What is the problem with many homes?

    2. What does T.H. Culhane do?

> Many homes use a lot of <u>energy</u> and water. This is bad for the <u>environment</u>. National Geographic Explorer T.H. Culhane teaches people to save energy and water. In the video, we visit his tiny home.

B With a partner, guess the answers to 1–3 below. Write ideas in your notebook. Then watch the video and check your answers.

    In Culhane's home, what things are in . . .

    1. the kitchen?   2. the living room?   3. the bedrooms?

    ❝ In the kitchen, there's a dishwasher . . .

C Read the sentences. Then watch the video again. Circle **T** for *true* or **F** for *false*. Correct the false statements.

    1. The kitchen appliances save energy.   **T**   **F**

    2. Most furniture in the home is new.   **T**   **F**

    3. The lights use very little energy.   **T**   **F**

    4. They grow a lot of their own food.   **T**   **F**

    5. They only dry clothes outside.   **T**   **F**

D How can you save energy and water at home? Read tips 1–6 and guess. Write a word in each blank.

    1. Turn off the _____ when you leave a room.

    2. Unplug your _____ and microwave.

    3. Use only LED ____lights____.

    4. Turn off the _____ when you brush your teeth.

    5. Start a _____ and grow some food.

    6. Don't buy everything _____. Buy some used furniture, too.

E Watch the video and check your answers in **D**. Do you do any of these things at home? Explain.

T.H. Culhane uses solar panels to power his home. He does other things to save energy, too.

Fashion bloggers gather for a boat trip in Istanbul.

GOALS **Lesson A**
/ Identify clothing items
/ Ask for and give prices of things

Lesson B
/ Describe clothing
/ Talk about personal style

CLOTHING

LOOK AT THE PHOTO. ANSWER THE QUESTIONS.

1. What colors do you see in the photo?
2. What are the women doing? Why are they doing it?

WARM-UP VIDEO

A Watch the first part of the video. Answer the questions with a partner.

　1. Who are the people in the video?

　2. Where do you think they are going?

B Read the list of words. Look up any words you don't know in your dictionary.

　☐ bags　　　　☐ headphones
　☐ boots　　　　☐ jeans
　☐ hats　　　　☐ sunglasses

C Watch the video. Check (✓) the things you see in **B**.

D Watch the video again. Answer the questions. Make a list with a partner.

　1. What other items of clothing do you see?

　2. Do you know the words in English?

E Answer the questions with a partner.

　1. Do you like the clothes you see in the video? Why or why not?

　2. How do people dress in your city? Is it similar to the way people dress in the video?

　　❝ My city is cold, so we never wear . . .

VOCABULARY

A Say the words with your teacher. Then talk about what you are wearing with a partner.

scarf · hat · gloves · jacket · T-shirt · shorts · pants · socks · sneakers · boots

B Look at the words in the box. Look up any words you don't know. Then answer the questions with a partner.

blouse	jeans	suit
dress	sandals	tie
heels	skirt	uniform

1. Which clothing items are for work?

2. Which ones are for relaxing at home?

C What do you wear at home? What do you wear at school? Tell a partner.

LISTENING

A Look at the Word Bank. What other words go with *a pair of*?

WORD BANK
a pair of shoes /
sunglasses / shorts

B **Listen for details.** M Jackson is a scientist. Listen. Answer the questions. 🎧88

1. Where does M Jackson go?
2. What does she study?
3. Who sometimes goes with her?

WORD BANK
cold
warm

C Listen again. Match each activity to the people. Then, in your notebook, write sentences about the people and their activities. 🎧88

1. enjoy the work
2. go down into ice caves
3. make podcasts   M Jackson
4. take photos   the students
5. travel around the world
6. wear a lot of clothing

D What clothing does M Jackson wear? Listen one more time and complete the list. 🎧88

1. two pairs of _____
2. a pair of _____
3. _____ pairs of _____
4. four _____

E Do you want to visit an ice cave? Why or why not?

A person stands in an ice cave in Iceland.

Galleria Alberto Sordi is a shopping center in a historic building in Rome. It's on Via del Corso, a great place to go shopping.

A Jin is from South Korea. He's in Rome on vacation. Listen. Then answer the questions. 🎧89

1. What is Jin doing?

2. What doesn't Jin want? How does he say that? Underline the words.

3. What does Jin buy? How does he say it? Circle the words.

Store Clerk: *Buon giorno.*

Jin: Um, hello. Do you speak English?

Store Clerk: Yes, I do. Can I help you?

Jin: Oh, yeah . . . thanks. I'm shopping for a gift for my sister.

Store Clerk: I see. Well, we have these nice silk scarves.

Jin: They're very pretty. How much are they?

Store Clerk: Sixty euros.

Jin: Sixty euros? OK, I'll think about it.

Store Clerk: We also have T-shirts . . . like this Roma one.

Jin: Oh, that's cool. How much is it?

Store Clerk: Nineteen euros.

Jin: That's perfect. I'll take it.

B Practice the conversation with a partner.

C Imagine you're on vacation in Italy. You want to buy a gift for someone. With a partner, make a new conversation.

- Shopper: Who are you shopping for? Tell the clerk.
- Store clerk: Show the shopper at least three items. Use the prices below. Try to make a sale!

  €300   €235   €95   €40   €35

D Switch roles and do **C** again.

SPEAKING STRATEGY 🎧90

Saying what you want

I'm looking for a gift for my sister.

Asking for and giving prices

How much are they?

  They're 60 euros.

OK, I'll think about it.

How much is the T-shirt?

  It's 19 euros.

I'll take it.

GRAMMAR

A Read the Unit 11, Lesson A Grammar Reference in the appendix. Complete the exercises. Then do the exercises below.

	Verb / Verb + *to*	Verb	Noun	
❶ She	has		winter boots.	
❷ She	has to	wear	four jackets	to go outside.
❸ He	wants		a silk scarf.	
❹ He	wants to	buy	a gift	for his sister.

HAVE TO AND WANT TO

B Read the sentences and answer the questions.

1. Which two sentences have the same meaning?

2. Which sentence means something is necessary?

   a. I want a new uniform.

   b. I have a new uniform.

   c. I want to buy a new uniform.

   d. I have to wear a new uniform.

C PRONUNCIATION: *Want to* and *have to* Work with a partner. Listen and repeat. Then complete the sentences with *want to* or *have to*. 🎧91

1. I _____ buy a new sweater. This one has a big hole in it.

2. I _____ visit Jamaica on my summer vacation.

3. You _____ dress up. You _____ wear a long dress.

4. I have free time now. Do you _____ do something?

D You are going skiing and need to pack for the trip. Discuss the questions with a partner.

boots	hat	sunglasses
camera	ski jacket	sweater
gloves	ski pants	two pairs of socks

1. Look at the packing list. What things do you already have? Which ones do you have to get?

2. What are three things that are not necessary, but that you want to pack anyway?

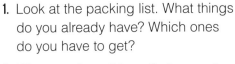

66 I don't have to take my own skis, but I want to pack them anyway.

At most ski areas, you can rent skis and poles for the day.

ACTIVE ENGLISH Try it out!

A Read the questions and think about your answers.

1. Do you buy many new clothes? Where do you shop? How much do you spend on jeans? T-shirts? shoes?

2. Complete this sentence: If you want to speak English well, you have to _____.

3. Look at three people in your class. What are they wearing?

4. What is something you want to do this year?

5. At school or work, do you have to wear a uniform? Are there clothes you cannot wear?

6. Which items of clothing are your favorites? Why?

7. Think about the clothes in your closet. What colors are they? Which colors do you look good in?

8. Describe traditional clothes in your culture. When do people wear them?

B Work with three or four other people.

1. Take turns. Choose a question from **A**.

2. Answer the question. If you can talk for one minute without stopping, you get one point.

3. Continue until there are no more questions. The winner is the person with the most points.

11A GOALS Now I can . . .

Identify clothing items _____

Ask for and give prices of things _____

1. Yes, I can.
2. Mostly, yes.
3. Not yet.

Women in Valencia, Spain, wear traditional dresses for the Festival de San Jose, held every spring.

VOCABULARY

A Look at the man in the photo with the black hat and the light blue suit. Read the sentences. Choose **T** for *true* or **F** for *false*.

1. The man's pants are **baggy**.   T   F
2. His jacket is **fitted**.   T   F
3. He looks **casual**.   T   F

B Use the words in **blue** from **A** to complete the Word Bank.

C Answer the questions. Make some notes.

1. When do you **dress up**?
2. Think about your own personal **style**. How do you describe it?
3. Do you like to be comfortable or **stylish**?

D Work with a partner. Ask and answer the questions in **C**.

" When do you dress up?

At the end of the year. Everyone in my family dresses up and we go out to dinner. "

Street fashion in Johannesburg, South Africa

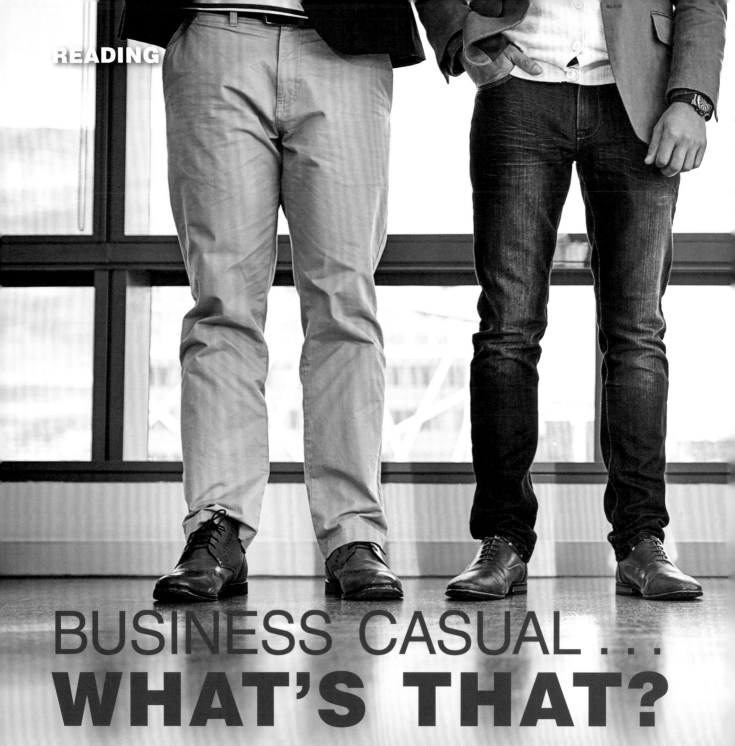

BUSINESS CASUAL ...
WHAT'S THAT?

What do people wear when they go to work every day? There isn't one easy answer to this question. The dress code (a set of style rules for a group of people) in one office is different from the dress code in another. But there is one style that is more popular at work these days. It's called "business casual." What is it exactly?

Business casual is a kind of dress code. It's not too dressy and not too casual. For men, it means "no suit," but also "no sneakers." In this style, men wear a nice dress shirt with a dark-colored jacket (for example, navy blue). They also wear dress pants in gray or light gray, but not black. A nice pair of jeans is OK, too. The pants aren't baggy. On their feet, they wear brown dress shoes and boots in the winter.

Women wear a nice blouse and a fitted jacket. The blouse covers their shoulders. They also wear nice dress pants, or jeans, or a medium-length skirt. On their feet, flats (comfortable shoes without heels) are OK, but flip-flops (light rubber sandals) are not.

Men say they like business casual because they don't have to wear a tie. Women like it, too—they don't have to wear heels. Business casual isn't too dressy. That's more comfortable for everyone. ◁92

Are these clothes acceptable for work?

A **Predict.** Look at the photo. Answer the questions.

1. Where are the people?

2. What are they wearing?

3. Look at the title. What do you think "business casual" is?

B Read the first two paragraphs. How is "business casual" described?

   a. It's the same in every company.

   b. It's not very popular today.

   c. It's between casual and dressy.

   d. It's not a dress code.

C Look at the photo again. Are the people wearing business casual? Find key words in the article to support your answer.

D Read the article. What do men and women usually wear to the office? Complete the chart. Then complete the tasks below.

	Men	**Women**
upper body		
lower body		
feet		

1. Name two things *not* to wear in the office: _____

2. Name two things you don't have to wear in the office: _____

E Discuss the questions with a partner.

1. What do you think of the business casual style? Do you see it in your country?

2. Is a dress code a good idea? Why or why not?

LISTENING

A In your opinion, what items are *not* appropriate for a job interview? Check (✓) your answers. Tell a partner.

☐ boots ☐ a T-shirt

☐ a hat ☐ a sweater

☐ a jacket ☐ sneakers

☐ jewelry ☐ a nice shirt or blouse

B Diego wants to get a job at his school. He's going to the interview now. What do you think he's wearing? Discuss with a partner.

C Diego and his sister are talking. What is Diego wearing right now? Listen. Match the words. 🎧93

1. brown a. pants

2. black b. tie

3. blue c. jacket

4. bright red d. shoes

5. light-colored e. shirt

D **Listen for detail and infer.** Listen again. How does Diego change his clothes? Write the new items below. Write "NC" for "no change." 🎧93

1. jacket ➔ _____

2. pants ➔ _____

3. shirt ➔ _____

4. tie ➔ _____

5. shoes ➔ _____

E How do you dress for an interview? What do you wear? Make some notes. Tell a partner.

upper body

_____

_____

lower body

_____

_____

Are these clothes good for an interview?

> **WORD BANK**
> When your clothes **match**, they have the same or a similar color and style.
> *Your shirt and your pants don't* **match**.

GRAMMAR

A Read the Unit 11, Lesson B Grammar Reference in the appendix. Complete the exercises. Then do the exercises below.

COUNT AND NONCOUNT NOUNS	
English divides nouns into things we can count (count nouns) and things we can't (noncount nouns).	
Count nouns are singular (= one thing) and plural (= two or more things). *I have four **ties**, but none of them match this **shirt***.	**Noncount nouns** only have a singular form. They don't have a plural form. *What kind of **jewelry** do you like?*
Use *a* or *an* before **singular count nouns**. *I need **a** new **jacket** for my interview.*	Don't use *a* or *an* before **noncount nouns**. *I need new **jewelry** for my interview.*
Use *some* for general amounts. Use it with **plural count nouns**. *I have **some** nice **skirts**.*	Use *some* with **noncount nouns**, too. *I need to buy **some** new **furniture**.*
Use *a pair of* to count things that are always plural (pants ➜ a pair of pants) You can also use *a pair of* to count things that come in sets of two (shoes ➜ a pair of shoes)	
Common noncount nouns: *furniture, information, jewelry, mail, money, music, vocabulary*	

B Read each sentence. Choose *OK* if the sentence is correct. Choose *Not OK* if it has an error.

OK / Not OK   **1.** Do you want to buy a new shoes?

_____

OK / Not OK   **2.** Do you like to wear bright colors?

_____

OK / Not OK   **3.** Do you wear school uniform?

_____

OK / Not OK   **4.** Do you sometimes wear a jewelry?

_____

OK / Not OK   **5.** What are some styles you like?

_____

OK / Not OK   **6.** Do you like a hip-hop music?

_____

OK / Not OK   **7.** Do you have a lot of homeworks?

_____

OK / Not OK   **8.** Is it easy for you to learn new vocabularies?

_____

C Work with a partner. Compare your answers. Rewrite the incorrect sentences to make them correct.

D Take turns. Ask and answer the questions in **B** with your partner.

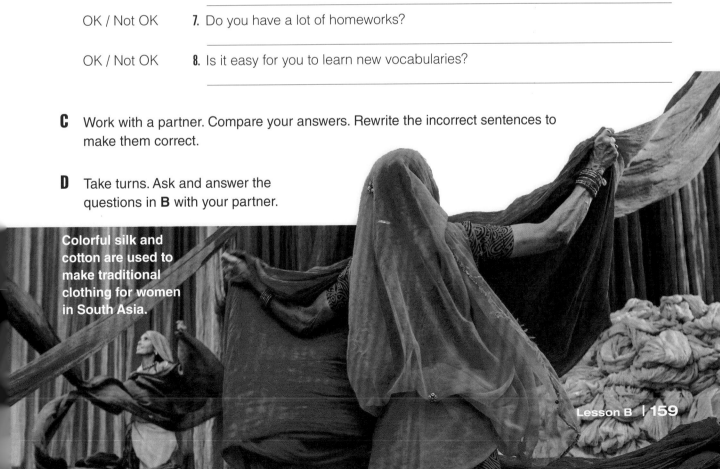

Colorful silk and cotton are used to make traditional clothing for women in South Asia.

ACTIVE ENGLISH Try it out!

A Look at the photo and read about Cristiano Ronaldo. Answer the questions. Discuss with a partner.

1. What is Cristiano Ronaldo's style?

2. Do you like it?

> Cristiano Ronaldo wears clothes from many different brands.
> For a casual look,* he likes to wear a nice pair of shoes, jeans, and a dress shirt.
> For a dressy look, he likes to wear a fitted suit with a tie.
> He looks good in a sweater or a leather bomber jacket with boots and a pair of sunglasses.
> He matches his shoes, pants, and shirts perfectly. He's stylish.
>
> *a casual **look** = a casual style

B Answer the questions.

1. Who do you follow on social media? _____

2. Talk about the person's casual and dressy looks. Make some notes.

   _____

   _____

3. What do you like about the person's style?

   _____

C **WRITING** Write about the person in **B**. Describe his or her style. Use the model in **A** to help you.

D Work with a partner. Take turns being Student A.

Student A: Tell your partner about your person's style.

Student B: Ask a follow-up question.

E Switch partners. Tell two more classmates about your person in **B**.

F As a class, write the names of five stylish people on the board. Take a vote. Who is the most stylish?

11B GOALS Now I can . . .

Describe clothing _____

Talk about personal style _____

1. Yes, I can.
2. Mostly, yes.
3. Not yet.

Cristiano Ronaldo is a famous soccer player. He sometimes wears a leather bomber jacket.

GLOBAL VOICES

A Look at the photo and read the caption. Then guess the answers to the questions.

   1. What is tweed? Choose the correct answers.

      a. It's a **rough and thick** / **soft and thin** fabric.

      b. It's **a cheap** / **an expensive** fabric.

   2. What do people usually make out of tweed? Cross out the one that doesn't belong.

      hats   jackets   shoes   skirts   suits

   3. The name of the video is *The Tweed Run*. What do you think the video is about?

B Watch the first part of the video. Check your answers in **A**.

C Watch the rest of the video. What do people do on the Tweed Run? Check (✓) your answers.

   ☐ have a dance party   ☐ have lunch   ☐ stop for tea

   ☐ have fun   ☐ meet new people   ☐ wear bright clothes

D Watch again. Match the words on the left (1–6) with the words on the right (a–e).

   1. stylish   **a.** bikes

   2. traditional   **b.** British clothing

   3. vintage   **c.** clothes

   4. beautiful   **d.** cycling event

   5. popular   **e.** fabric

   6. casual

E Think about a festival or event you know. Prepare to tell a partner about it. Answer the questions. Make some notes.

   1. What clothes do people wear?

   2. Do you like to join in?

F Talk for 30–45 seconds. Tell a partner about the festival or event.

Stylish bicyclists on the streets of London

12

JOBS

LOOK AT THE PHOTO. ANSWER THE QUESTIONS.

1. What is the man's job? Is this job hard or easy?

2. Do you want to do a job like this? Why or why not?

WARM-UP VIDEO

A Read the information below. In your country, do students have Career Day? Tell a partner.

> The video is about Career Day in the US. On Career Day, young students give a short presentation to their classmates about a job they want to do in the future.

B Look at the jobs below and say them with your teacher. Which do you know? Look up the ones you don't know in a dictionary.

☐ an actress   ☐ a photographer

☐ a baseball player   ☐ the president

☐ a doctor   ☐ a soccer player

☐ a filmmaker   ☐ a surfer

☐ a graphic designer   ☐ a teacher

☐ a musician   ☐ a veterinarian

C Watch the video with the sound off. What jobs do the students want to do in the future? Check (✓) the jobs in **B**.

D Watch the video with the sound on. Check your answers in **B**.

E Which job(s) in **B** are interesting to you? Tell a partner.

A sound engineer tests
the noise made by a
hair dryer.

GOALS

Lesson A

/ Identify different jobs

/ Talk about your job

Lesson B

/ Explain your work goals

/ Talk about things you can and can't do

WHAT DO YOU DO?

VOCABULARY

A Say the jobs with your teacher. Look up new words in your dictionary.

business	healthcare	law and safety
manager*	dentist	lawyer
receptionist	doctor	police officer
salesperson	_____	_____

restaurant	technology	travel and hospitality
chef	_____	flight attendant
_____	IT manager	hotel desk clerk*
server (waiter / waitress)	software developer	_____

> **i** Notice: Many jobs end in -er, -or, or -ist.

*different types:
   office / sales / store **manager**
   desk / store **clerk**

B Say the jobs below with your teacher and think about their meanings. Then write each job in the chart in **A** with a partner.

cook   engineer   nurse   salesperson   security guard   tour guide

C Choose five jobs from **A** and **B**. Then act them out for your partner. Your partner guesses the jobs.

D Answer the questions with a partner.

1. Which jobs in the chart . . .

   • require English? (You have to use English.)

   • make the most money?

   • are interesting to you?

   " In a big hotel, a desk clerk has to use English.

2. Do you know anyone with these jobs?

   " My dad is a . . .

Joy Buolamwini is a computer scientist. She studies the use of artificial intelligence (AI) in our daily lives.

LISTENING

A Look at the photo. What job is the robot doing? Tell a partner.

B **Listen for the main idea.** Read the sentence. Then listen and choose the correct answer. 🎧94

The talk is about why _____ robots in the workplace.

a. we need more

b. there aren't many

c. people like and don't like

C Which jobs are robots doing these days? Listen again and circle the answers. 🎧94

a. cleaner

b. doctor

c. manager

d. nurse

e. nurse's aide

f. receptionist

g. security guard

h. server

i. software developer

j. teacher

D Listen. For Job 1, write the robot's job. For the question, check (✓) the correct answer(s). 🎧95

	The robot's job	What does the robot do?
Job 1		☐ works slowly ☐ cleans rooms ☐ tells people to go faster
Job 2		☐ cleans rooms ☐ brings things ☐ teaches people

E Listen and complete Job 2 in **D**. 🎧96

F What do you think about robots in the workplace? Explain your opinion to a partner.

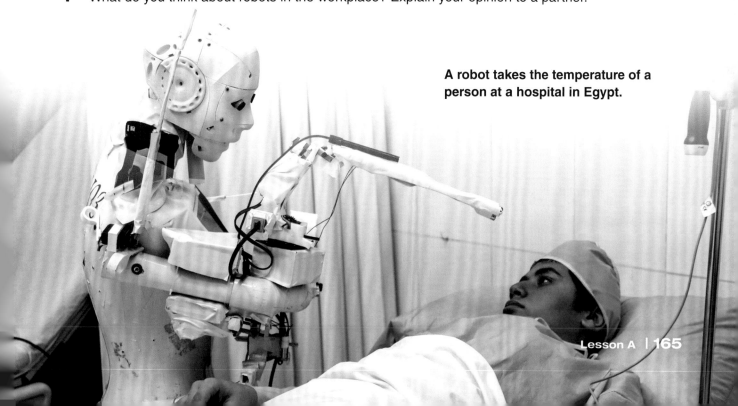

A robot takes the temperature of a person at a hospital in Egypt.

SPEAKING

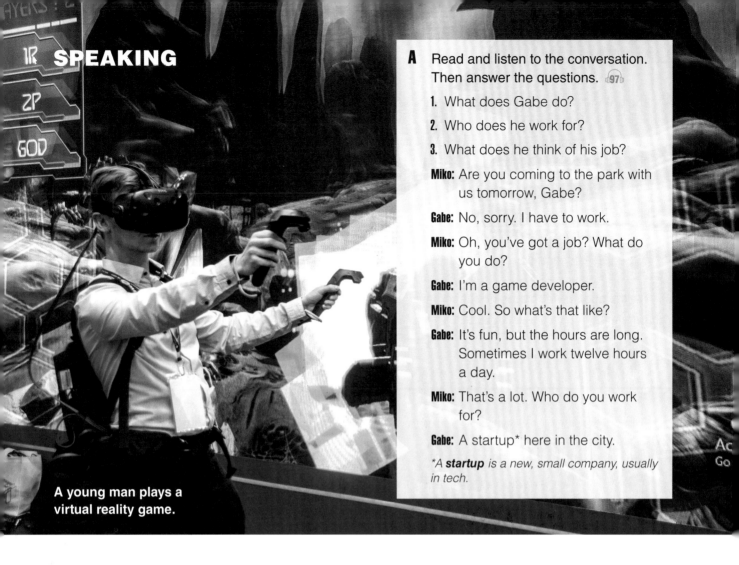

A young man plays a
virtual reality game.

A Read and listen to the conversation.
Then answer the questions. 🎧97

1. What does Gabe do?

2. Who does he work for?

3. What does he think of his job?

Miko: Are you coming to the park with
us tomorrow, Gabe?

Gabe: No, sorry. I have to work.

Miko: Oh, you've got a job? What do
you do?

Gabe: I'm a game developer.

Miko: Cool. So what's that like?

Gabe: It's fun, but the hours are long.
Sometimes I work twelve hours
a day.

Miko: That's a lot. Who do you work
for?

Gabe: A startup* here in the city.

*A **startup** is a new, small company, usually
in tech.

B PRONUNCIATION: Question word + *do* + *you* Listen again to the questions and answers.
Then say them with a partner. 🎧98

A: What do you do?
B: I'm a game developer.

A: Who do you work for?
B: A startup here in the city.

C Practice the conversation in **A** with a partner.

D Review the Speaking Strategy. Then complete the
conversations with the correct forms of the words in bold.

1. **A:** What _____ you do?

   B: _____ a flight attendant.
   I _____ Korean Air.

2. **A:** What _____ your brother do?

   B: He _____ an office.

SPEAKING STRATEGY 🎧99
Talking about jobs

What do you do?	**I'm**	a game developer / an office manager.
	I work in	a hotel / a bank / a cafe.
	I work for	Apple / Toyota.

E Interview five classmates about their jobs. Take notes.

❝ What do you do?

I'm a . . . I work . . . ❞

❝ What do you do?

I . . . now, but I want to be a . . . in the future. ❞

F Compare your answers in **E** with a partner. What are popular answers?

GRAMMAR

A Read the Unit 12, Lesson A Grammar Reference in the appendix. Complete the exercises. Then do the exercises below.

QUESTIONS WITH *LIKE*	
A: I'm a game developer.	**A:** My coworker is from Brazil.
B: Really? **What's** that **like**?	**B:** Oh? **What's** he **like**?
A: It's fun, but the hours are long.	**A:** He's nice.

B Say the words in the chart below with your teacher. Then answer the questions with a partner.

1. Which words do you know? Look up new words in your dictionary.

2. Does each word have a positive or negative meaning?

Describe jobs		Describe people	
boring	hard	boring	helpful
cool	interesting	friendly / nice	kind
easy	rewarding*	fun	lazy
fun	stressful	hardworking	smart

*A **rewarding** job makes you feel good.

C Choose the correct answers. Then practice the conversation with a partner.

> **i** To make adjectives stronger
> My job is <u>very</u> **hard**.
> **To make adjectives softer**
> My job is <u>kind of</u> **hard**.

A: What do you do?

B: I **work for** / **work in** a call center.

A: Really? What's **that** / **he** like?

B: It's kind of **easy** / **hard**. I have to answer questions eight hours a day.

A: Sounds **fun** / **stressful**. What **your coworkers are** / **are your coworkers** like?

B: They're **fun** / **boring**. We laugh a lot together.

D Work with a partner. Complete the task.

1. Choose three jobs from the Vocabulary page, or think of your own jobs.

2. Describe each job: What is it like? What are the people like? Where do people with these jobs sometimes work? Write ideas in your notebook.

3. Tell another pair your ideas. Do you agree with theirs?

> " A doctor's job isn't easy, but it's usually rewarding. Doctors help people.
>
> Many doctors are very smart. "

Workers install LED lights on the side of a building in Hanoi, Vietnam.

A Look at the business card with your class. What information is on it?

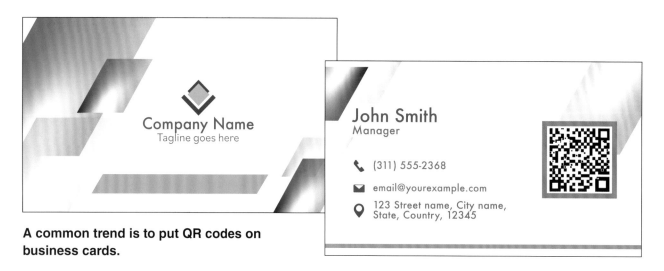

A common trend is to put QR codes on business cards.

John Smith
Manager

☎ (311) 555-2368

✉ email@yourexample.com

📍 123 Street name, City name,
State, Country, 12345

B Work on your own.

1. Think of your dream job. Make three identical business cards on three pieces of paper.

2. Answer the questions below about your job.

	Me	Partner 1	Partner 2	Partner 3
What do you do?				
Who do you work for?				
What's your job like?				

C Imagine you are at a party. Introduce yourself to three people. Give each person your business card. Then complete the chart in **B** with information about each person you meet.

❝ So, what do you do?
I'm a . . . ❞

❝ Sounds interesting. Who do you work for?
A startup called . . . Here's my card. ❞

D Which person has the most interesting job? Tell the class.

12A GOALS Now I can . . .

Identify different jobs _____

Talk about my job _____

1. Yes, I can.
2. Mostly, yes.
3. Not yet.

VOCABULARY

A Look up the words *experience* and *goal* in your dictionary. Then answer the questions with a partner.

1. In your city, can young people get jobs easily?

2. Read only the goal and the problem below. What is the goal? What can you do about the problem? Think of some ideas.

> **How to Get a Job without Experience**
>
> **Your goal:** You want to **get a full-time job** with a company.
>
> **Your problem:** You're a student. You don't **have** any work **experience**.
>
> **What can you do?**
>
> 1. Try to **get a part-time job** with the company. Work there 15 hours a week and **get** some **experience**.
>
> 2. **Do an internship.** You can learn a lot, but there's usually no **pay**. You don't **make money**, but you **get experience** and meet people.

B Now read all the information in the box in **A**. In your opinion, are the two ideas good? Why or why not? Tell a partner.

C What are your future work goals? Complete 1–3. Then tell a partner. Are your goals the same?

1. I want to get _____.
   ☐ a full-time job   ☐ a different job
   ☐ a part-time job   ☐ some work experience

2. I want to work for _____.

   I want to do an internship at _____.

3. Pay: I want to make _____ a month / a year.

WORD BANK
1,000 (one **thousand**)
1,000,000 (one **million**)

 I want to get a part-time job this summer.

In the future, I want to make $60,000 a year. 99

Over 90% of companies say a person must have work experience to get hired.

WORKING IN TWO
LANGUAGES

In the world today, it helps to be bilingual. When you speak two languages, you have more choices. You can get a job in many different fields.[1] In this article, we look at two of them.

Travel & Tourism

Across the world, one in every ten jobs today is in travel and tourism. Millions of people work in this field, and many of <u>them</u> are bilingual.

The jobs with the best pay are usually in management. Bilingual hotel and sales managers, for example, can make good money. Some managers have hospitality degrees.

But many others start in different jobs (for example, hotel clerk). They get experience and then, in time, they work their way up into management.

Healthcare

Today, there is a nursing shortage. Worldwide, there are about 28 million nurses, and we need almost six million more. In big cities in a number of countries, hospitals especially need bilingual nurses. Nursing jobs are different from many travel and tourism jobs: you need a degree to get one. 🎧100🎧

[1] A **field** is an area of work or study (business, healthcare, technology, etc.).
[2] **Customer service representatives** answer people's questions and help with problems online or by phone.

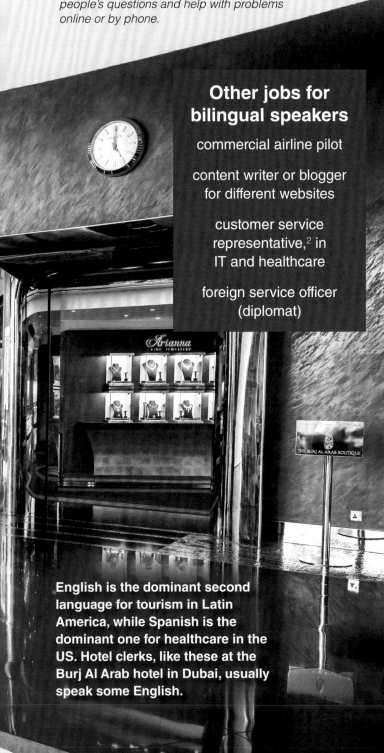

Other jobs for bilingual speakers

commercial airline pilot

content writer or blogger for different websites

customer service representative,[2] in IT and healthcare

foreign service officer (diplomat)

English is the dominant second language for tourism in Latin America, while Spanish is the dominant one for healthcare in the US. Hotel clerks, like these at the Burj Al Arab hotel in Dubai, usually speak some English.

A **Skim and predict.** Read the title, the first paragraph, and the headings in **bold**. Also look quickly at any key words in the article. Answer the questions with a partner.

1. What is the reading mainly about?
2. What jobs do you expect to read about?

B Read the article and check your ideas in **A**.

C Find the underlined words in the article. Then choose the correct answers below.

1. The word *them* means **workers** / **jobs** in travel and tourism.
2. When people *work their way up*, they start in one job and then **stay in that job** / **move to a higher job**.
3. When there is a *shortage*, there **isn't enough** / **is a lot** of something.
4. The word *one* means a **tourism** / **nursing** job.

D **Scan.** Work with a partner. Answer the questions.

Student A: Talk about tourism jobs.

1. How many people work in the field?
2. What are some of the best jobs? Why?
3. Do you need a degree to do these jobs?

Student B: Talk about nursing.

4. How many people do the job?
5. Where are bilingual nurses needed the most?
6. Do you need a degree to do the job?

E With a partner, choose a job from the list of other jobs for bilingual speakers or think of your own. Learn about it together. Then tell another pair about it.

- In the job, what does a person do?
- Is the pay good?
- Do you need a degree to do the job?
- Imagine you want to get the job. How can you do it?

To make some extra money, this person walks dogs as a side hustle.

A **Predict.** Look at the photo and read the caption. Then read the sentence below. Guess the answers.

A side hustle is _____.

a. a full-time job   c. a job you do for a company

b. a part-time job   d. often a person's hobby

B Listen and check your ideas in **A**. Circle the correct answers. 🎧101

C With a partner, try to guess some of the answers below. Look up new words.

WORD BANK

A *hobby* is a fun activity you do in your free time.

Tutoring is teaching.

Popular Side Hustles

1. **Beauty and Fashion**
   • hairstylist
   • makeup _____
   • personal _____

2. **Tutoring and Teaching**
   • _____ or science
   • _____
   • cooking

3. **Making and Selling Things**
   • _____
   • _____
   • things for the home

D Listen and complete 1–3 in **C**. Write a word in each blank. 🎧102

E Answer the questions with a partner.

1. Can you think of other side hustles? Can you make money doing these things?

2. What side hustles can you do with English?

" My friend is a DJ on weekends. He makes good money.

GRAMMAR

A Read the Unit 12, Lesson B Grammar Reference in the appendix. Complete the exercises. Then do the exercises below.

TALKING ABOUT ABILITY WITH *CAN* / *CAN'T*		
Yes / *No* questions	**Can** you speak French?	Yes, **I can**. / No, I *can't*.
Wh- questions	Which languages **can** you speak?	(I **can** speak) Spanish and English.
	Who **can** speak Japanese?	Toshi (**can**).

B Read the job ad. Then complete the interview questions below. Write three *Yes* / *No* questions and two *Wh-* questions with *can*.

> We're looking for hardworking, friendly tour guides to take groups of people to interesting areas around the city.
>
> Start date: early summer
>
> Please be able to speak English, work full time, and walk for long periods.

Yes / No question

1a. Can you work this summer?

2a. Can _____ English?

3a. _____ full time?

4a. _____ ?

Follow-up *Wh-* question

1b. When can you start?

2b. How well can you speak it?

3b. What days _____ ?

4b. _____ ?

C Ask a partner the interview questions in **B**. Is your partner a good person for the job?

" Can you work this summer?

Yes, I can. "

" When can you start?

In June. "

D Think of a job and make a new ad with your partner. Then write four interview questions with *can*.

E Work with another pair. Complete the task.

1. Show them your job ad and questions. Read theirs.

2. Use your questions and interview one person from the other pair for your job. Your partner does the same. Take notes on the other person's answers.

3. Compare notes with your partner. Which person is best for your job? Why?

A tricycle tour guide in Mexico City

ACTIVE ENGLISH Try it out!

A Read the questions in the chart. Think about your answers.

Can you . . .

___ speak and write well?	___ play an instrument?	___ run a long distance?
___ remember information easily?	___ read or write music?	___ play a sport well?
___ tell interesting stories?	___ sing well?	___ dance well?

Group 1 Total: _____   Group 3 Total: _____   Group 5 Total: _____

___ solve problems quickly?	___ fix or make things?	___ give good advice?
___ play chess well?	___ draw or paint well?	___ talk to new people easily?
___ do math quickly in your head?	___ take interesting photos?	___ understand others' feelings?

Group 2 Total: _____   Group 4 Total: _____   Group 6 Total: _____

B Ask a partner the questions in **A**. Use *Can you . . .* . For your partner's answers, write a number:

3 = Yes, I can.   2 = Yes, a little.   1 = No, I can't.

> " Can you play an instrument?
>
> Yes, I can. "

C Now add the points for each group in **A** and write the totals.
Then look at the jobs charts on page 216. What are good jobs for your partner?

D Look again at the chart in **A**. When did your partner say, "Yes, I can"? Ask your partner questions about these abilities.

> " What instrument can you play?
>
> I can play the violin. "

E Read the paragraph. Then answer the questions with a partner.

My work goals

I like comics and I can draw well. I usually draw my own characters. I practice every day. Right now, I'm majoring in graphic design. In the future, I want to be a video game developer. Maybe I can do an internship first. Then I can get a full-time job and work for a big animation company. That's my goal.

---

1. What can he do well?

2. What are his goals? What does he want to be?

F **WRITING** Write about your work goals. Answer the questions in **E** about yourself. Then exchange papers with a partner and answer the questions in **E** about your partner.

12B GOALS   Now I can . . .

Explain my work goals _____

Talk about things I can and can't do _____

1. Yes, I can.

2. Mostly, yes.

3. Not yet.

GLOBAL VOICES

A Look at the photo and read the caption. Where does Corey Arnold work? What do you know about these places? Tell a partner.

B In the video, Corey Arnold answers questions 1–3. Guess his two answers to each question. Then watch the video and check your ideas.

1. What do you do?

    a. I'm a photographer.

    b. I'm a fisherman.

    c. I'm a tour guide.

2. Who do you work for?

    a. my family's company

    b. myself

    c. many different companies

3. What's your job like?

    a. Busy. I travel often.

    b. It's kind of boring sometimes.

    c. It can be difficult and dangerous.

WORD BANK

A *freelancer* works for themself and does different jobs.

An *organization* is a large company.

C What do you think of Corey's job? What is it like? Is it interesting to you? Why or why not? Tell a partner.

D In your notebook, answer the questions in **B**. You can talk about yourself or take the role of a famous person.

E Work with a partner. Complete the task.

1. **Student A:** Ask your partner questions 1–3. At the end, ask two follow-up questions to learn more.

    Student B: Close your notebook and answer the questions.

2. Switch roles and repeat step 1.

National Geographic Explorer Corey Arnold often works in Alaska and the Arctic.

REAL WORLD LINK THE NEXT BIG THING

He Liangcai rides his motorized suitcase around Changsha, China.

A Read about an American TV show below. Then answer the questions with a partner.

Shark Tank is a popular TV show. On it, there are two types of people: inventors and sharks. The inventors are people with ideas for new and interesting products. On the show, they explain their ideas to a group of experienced businesspeople (the sharks).

The sharks give money to the inventors with the best ideas. Then these inventors can make their products and sell them. When the products make money, the sharks do, too.

1. On the show, who are the inventors? What is their goal?

2. Who are the sharks? What do they do?

3. Look at the photo. Is it a good product? Why or why not?

B Read the sentence below and guess the answers with a partner. Then listen and check your ideas. Are you surprised? 🎧103🎧

Two of the best-selling products ever on *Shark Tank* are _____ and _____.

a. a chair for the office

c. a kitchen sponge

b. socks

d. a pair of sneakers

66 No way! The answers are . . .

C Write the two products from **B** on the lines. Then read 1–6. Listen and write your answers. 🎧104

Product 1: _____

1. What's the problem with the old product?
   They're uncomfortable: They're
   too _____ or too _____.

2. What's the new product like?
   They're very comfortable.
   They last a _____ time.
   They come in _____ colors.

3. How much are they?
   $ _____ or more for a casual
   pair

Product 2: _____

4. What's the problem with the old product?
   It doesn't _____ well
   in _____ water. It's too
   _____ to hold.

5. What's the new product like?
   It changes in _____ water,
   so it _____ better. It's
   _____, so it's comfortable to
   hold. It lasts a _____ time.

6. How much is it?
   $ _____ for a pack of four

D Check your answers in **C** with a partner. Are they good products? Why or why not?

E With a partner, design your own product. Choose an idea from the box.
Then answer questions 1–3 in your notebook.

1. Is your product . . .

   • a type of clothing? What kind?

   • for a room in the house? Which one?

   • something people use at work? Which job?

2. Describe your product: What does it do? How can it help people?
   Are there similar products? If yes, how is yours better?

3. How much is it? Can most people buy it?

> Your product can be . . .
>
> • a type of clothing.
>
> • for the home.
>
> • for the workplace.
>
> • your own idea.

F **You Choose** Choose an option to present your product.

Option 1: Draw a picture of your product. Write a short ad to explain it.

Option 2: Make a video. Show and explain your product.

Option 3: Make a 3-panel display board. Show and explain your product.

> **Your goal:** You
> want people to like
> your product! You
> have five minutes to
> present it.

G Present your product and learn about others. Follow the steps.

1. Join another pair. Present your product.

2. When you listen, answer questions 1–3 in **E** in your
   notebook about the other pair's product. You can
   also ask questions.

3. Repeat steps 1 and 2 with two other pairs.

> 66 Is your closet messy? With our product . . .
>
> Do you work in an office? With our
> product, you can exercise at your desk. 99

H Look at the three products you learned about in **G**. You can give money to one. Complete the
sentence and tell the class. Which product is the most popular?

I want to give my money to . . .

LANGUAGE SUMMARIES

UNIT 1: INTRODUCTIONS

LESSON A	LESSON B
Vocabulary	**Vocabulary**
first name　　　email address	**be into** (something)
last name　　　nickname	
	favorite
letters of the alphabet:　numbers 0–10: zero,	
A B C D E F G H I J　one, two, three, four,	**movie**
K L M N O P Q R S　five, six, seven, eight,	**music** (**classical**, **dance**,
T U V W X Y Z　nine, ten	**hip-hop** / **rap**, **pop**)
phone number	**singer** / **band**
	sport (**baseball**, **basketball**, **soccer**,
@ = at	**swimming**)
.com = dot com	**sports team** / **player**
.edu = dot e-d-u	**TV show**

Speaking Strategy

Introducing yourself

Hi. What's your name?

　My name is . . . / I'm . . .

(It's) nice to meet you.

　(It's) nice to meet you, too.

UNIT 2: COUNTRIES

LESSON A	LESSON B
Vocabulary	**Vocabulary**
country　　　　　　　　　(capital) city	**beautiful**
nationality	**big** / **large** ↔ **small**
	busy
Australia → **Australian**	**crowded**
Brazil → **Brazilian**	**exciting**
China → **Chinese**	**famous**
Japan → **Japanese**	**friendly**
Korea → **Korean**	**fun**
Mexico → **Mexican**	**interesting** ↔ **boring**
Peru → **Peruvian**	**old** ↔ **new**
Portugal → **Portuguese**	**popular**
Spain → **Spanish**	**relaxing**
Turkey → **Turkish**	**tall**
the United Kingdom (**the UK**) → **British**	**wonderful**
the United States (**the US**) → **American**	

Speaking Strategy

Asking where someone is from

Where are you from?	Really? Where exactly?
(I'm from) Japan.	(I'm from) a small town near Tokyo.
Really? Which city?	Are you from Colombia?
(I'm from) Tokyo.	Yes, I am. / No, I'm from Peru.

UNIT 3: POSSESSIONS

LESSON A		LESSON B
Vocabulary		**Vocabulary**
backpack	birthday	**clean** ↔ **messy**
gift card	expensive	**easy** ↔ **hard**
headphones		**expensive** ↔ **cheap**
laptop		**good** ↔ **bad**
movie tickets		**important** ↔ **unimportant**
sunglasses		
wallet		
watch		

Speaking Strategy
Giving and Replying to Thanks
  Saying *Thank You*
  Thank you very much.
  Thank you.
  Thanks a lot.
  Thanks.

Replies
You're welcome.
My pleasure.
Sure, no problem.
You bet.

UNIT 4: ACTIVITIES

LESSON A	LESSON B
Vocabulary **drink** (soda) do homework **eat** (pizza) run **exercise** wait for (a person, a bus) **go** (to school) **listen** (to music) **shop** **study** (for a test) **talk** (on the phone) **text** (a friend) **watch** (TV)	**Vocabulary** **art** **business** **engineering** **graphic design** **history** **hospitality** **information technology (IT)** **law** **math** **nursing** **science** **go to** (college) **major in** (art / math) **plan to** (do something) **prepare for** **study** (business / nursing) **take a(n) . . . class**

Speaking Strategy

Greeting people and asking how they are

Positive response ☺	**Negative response** ☹
A: Hi, . . . How are you doing? **B:** Fine. / OK. / All right. / Pretty good. How about you? **A:** I'm fine.	**A:** Hi, . . . How are you doing? **B:** So-so. **A:** Yeah? What's wrong? **B:** I'm waiting for the bus. It's late!

UNIT 5: FOOD

LESSON A

Vocabulary

beans
bread
burger
cheese
(fried) chicken
coffee
fries
fruit
juice
onions
pasta
(baked) potato
rice
(spinach) salad
(tuna fish) sandwich
soda
(vegetable) soup
steak
tea
tomato (sauce)
water

snack

breakfast
lunch
dinner

spicy

LESSON B

Vocabulary

energy
good for you ↔ bad for you
healthy ↔ unhealthy
high in ↔ low in (sugar)
meals
taste (good / bad)

Speaking Strategy

Talking about likes and dislikes

Do you like Indian food?
  I love it!
  Yeah, I like it.
  It's OK, but it's not my favorite.
  Not really.

UNIT 6: RELATIONSHIPS

LESSON A

Vocabulary
- **aunt**
- **brother**
- **cousin**
- **daughter**
- **father / dad**
- **grandfather**
- **grandmother**
- **grandparents**
- **husband – wife**
- **mother / mom**
- **nephew – niece**
- **parents**
- **sister**
- **son**
- **uncle**

10 ten	24 twenty-four
11 eleven	25 twenty-five
12 twelve	26 twenty-six
13 thirteen	27 twenty-seven
14 fourteen	28 twenty-eight
15 fifteen	29 twenty-nine
16 sixteen	30 thirty
17 seventeen	40 forty
18 eighteen	50 fifty
19 nineteen	60 sixty
20 twenty	70 seventy
21 twenty-one	80 eighty
22 twenty-two	90 ninety
23 twenty-three	100 one hundred

grandma
older ↔ younger (brother, sister)
look alike

daughter
son

stepmother

LESSON B

Vocabulary
- **(be / get) married**
- **(be) seeing someone**
- **(be) single**

- **boyfriend**
- **couple**
- **girlfriend**

meet (someone)

in (your) twenties

Speaking Strategy
Talking about age
How old is your sister?
  (She's) 18.
How old are you?
  (I'm) 22.
Are you the same age?
  Yes, we're both 20.
  No, he's older. He's 24.
  No, he's younger. He's 18.

UNIT 7: TIME

LESSON A	LESSON B
Vocabulary	**Vocabulary**
one o'clock	**go**
one-fifteen / a quarter past one	**biking**
one thirty / half past one	**driving**
one forty-five / a quarter to two	**running**
early ↔ late	**go for**
	a bike ride
wake up	**a drive**
take a shower	**a run**
get dressed	
leave home	**go to**
go to school	**a concert**
start (class)	**a friend's house**
finish (class)	**the movies**
go home	
go to bed	**weekend**

in the morning
~ afternoon
~ evening

Speaking Strategy
Making and responding to suggestions

Making a suggestion	**Saying yes**	**Saying no politely**
Let's go to the park.	(That's a) good idea.	I don't really like
We could see a movie.	(That's a) great idea.	action movies.
How about an action movie?	(That) sounds good.	

UNIT 8: SPECIAL OCCASIONS

LESSON A	LESSON B
Vocabulary	Vocabulary
January	attend
February	celebrate
March	compete
April	event
May	every (day / week / month / year)
June	festival
July	parade
August	perform
September	take place
October	traditional
November	
December	
winter	
spring	
summer	
fall	
week	
month	
year	

Speaking Strategy
Saying you know or don't know something
Is today a holiday?

Yes, it is. / No, it isn't.	(certain)
Maybe.	(less certain)
I'm not sure.	(not certain at all)
I don't know.	(don't know)
I have no idea.	

UNIT 9: TOGETHER

LESSON A

Vocabulary

chore
clean (a room)
do the dishes
do the laundry
make breakfast / dinner
make your bed
take out the garbage

do homework
make a list
make noise

loud
pay the rent

always
usually
often
sometimes
hardly ever
never

LESSON B

Vocabulary

friend
  best ~
  close ~
  good ~
  old ~

friendship
get along
hang out
keep in touch
make friends

remember ↔ forget

Speaking Strategy
Apologizing
Making an apology
(I'm) sorry.
(I'm) sorry about that.
I'm really sorry. [stronger]

Responding to an apology
No problem.
That's OK / all right.
Don't worry about it.

UNIT 10: HOME

LESSON A

Vocabulary

apartment
bathroom
bathtub
bed
bedroom
chair
closet
dining area
kitchen
living room
shower
sofa
table

ground floor
live in (an apartment)
live on (the third) floor

AC (air conditioning)
elevator
microwave (oven)
refrigerator
rent
stairs
up ↔ down
window

LESSON B

Vocabulary

color

black
(dark / light) blue
brown
gray
green
orange
pink
purple
red
white
(bright) yellow

happy ↔ unhappy, sad
relaxed ↔ nervous,
  uncomfortable

furniture
space

Speaking Strategy
Showing surprise
There's no elevator, and I'm on the fifth floor.

Really? / Are you serious?
You're kidding. / No way.

UNIT 11: CLOTHING

LESSON A

Vocabulary

blouse	a pair of
boots	~ shoes
dress	~ shorts
gloves	~ sunglasses
hat	
heels	
jacket	
jeans	
pants	
sandals	
scarf	
shorts	
skirt	
sneakers	
socks	
suit	
T-shirt	
tie	
uniform	

LESSON B

Vocabulary

baggy / loose ↔ fitted / tight   match (v)
casual ↔ dressy
dress up
style
stylish

Speaking Strategy
Saying what you want
I'm looking for a gift for my sister.

Asking for and giving prices
How much are they?
  They're 60 euros.
OK, I'll think about it.

How much is the T-shirt?
  It's 19 euros.
I'll take it.

UNIT 12: JOBS

LESSON A	LESSON B
Vocabulary chef cook dentist doctor engineer flight attendant hotel desk clerk IT manager lawyer manager nurse police officer receptionist salesperson security guard server (**waiter** / **waitress**) software developer tour guide	Vocabulary do an internship get a (part-time ↔ full-time) job get / have experience goal make money pay 1,000 (one **thousand**) 1,000,000 (one **million**)

Speaking Strategy
Talking about jobs
What do you do?
   I'm a game developer / an office manager.
   I work in a hotel / a bank / a cafe.
   I work for Apple / Toyota.

1 INTRODUCTIONS

LESSON A

SUBJECT PRONOUNS WITH *BE*			
Pronoun	***Be***		**Contractions with *be***
I	am		I am = I'm
You	are	a student.	you are = you're
He / She	is		he is = he's / she is = she's
We / They	are	students.	we are = we're / they are = they're
It	is	a book.	it is = it's

i In speaking, use contractions.

POSSESSIVE ADJECTIVES WITH *BE*			
Possessive adjective		***Be***	
My			
Your			
His / Her	last name	**is**	Cruz.
Our / Their			
Its	title	**is**	*World Link*.

A Complete each sentence with the correct form of the verb *be*.

1. She _____ a teacher.
2. It _____ a book.
3. You _____ my classmate.
4. I _____ at school.

B Look at the underlined words. Then write the correct subject pronoun.

1. <u>Mei and Beto</u> are here.
   _____ are here.
2. <u>My book</u> is at home.
   _____ is at home.
3. <u>Sofia</u> is at school.
   _____ is at school.
4. <u>Carlos</u> is at home.
   _____ is at home.

C Complete the sentences with the correct subject pronoun or possessive adjective.

1. _____ is a teacher. _____ name is Mr. Porter.
2. _____ are my classmates. _____ names are Beto and Mei.
3. We're classmates. _____ names are Alma and Min.
4. _____ is a teacher. _____ name is Ms. Garcia.

D Rewrite each sentence in your notebook. Use a contraction.

1. I am a student.
2. You are my classmate.
3. She is a teacher.
4. It is my nickname.
5. They are my classmates.
6. He is a student.

LESSON B

YES / NO QUESTIONS WITH BE			SHORT ANSWERS	
Be	**Pronoun**		**Affirmative**	**Negative**
Am	I	in this class?	Yes, you **are**.	No, you're **not**.* / No, you **aren't**.
Are	you	a student?	Yes, I **am**.	No, I'm **not**.
Is	he / she		Yes, he / she **is**.	No, he's **not**.* / No, she **isn't**.
Is	it	your favorite team?	Yes, it **is**.	No, it's **not**.* / No, it **isn't**.
Are	we	in this class?	Yes, we **are**.	No, we're **not**.* / No, we **aren't**.
Are	they	pop singers?	Yes, they **are**.	No, they're **not**.* / No, they **aren't**.

In spoken English, this negative form is more common.

A Read each question. Choose the correct answer.

1. Is your name Alma?   a. No, it's not.   b. No, I'm not.

2. Are you from Canada?   a. No, you're not.   b. No, I'm not.

3. Is Ms. Kim the teacher?   a. Yes, she is.   b. Yes, it is.

4. Are you friends with Jane?   a. Yes, I am.   b. Yes, I'm friends.

5. Am I late for class?   a. No, it's not.   b. No, you aren't.

6. Are Mei and Beto your classmates?   a. Yes, we are.   b. No, they're not.

Haru Tanaka

His friends Sofia and Milo

B Look at the photos above. Complete the questions and answers.

1. __Is__ his last name Sato?   __No__, it _'s not / isn't_. It's Tanaka.

2. _____ baseball _____ sport?   No, _____. _____ is his favorite.

3. _____ Sofia and Milo his friends?   _____.

4. _____ they all students?   No, _____. Haru is a soccer player.

5. _____ Sofia Haru's girlfriend?   _____. They're just friends.

6. _____ you friends with Haru?   Yes, _____.

COUNTRIES

LESSON A

QUESTIONS WITH *WHO*			ANSWERS	
Who	is 's	he / she?	He's / She's my classmate.	*Who* asks about people.
		from Mexico? with you?	Tomas (is).	
	are	you? they?	(I'm) Sara. (They're) my friends.	

QUESTIONS WITH *WHERE*			ANSWERS	
Where	are	you / they?	(I'm / We're / They're) **at** school / work / home. **at** the beach / a museum.	*Where* asks about a place. Use *at* + a place. Use *in* / *from* + a city or country.
Where	is 's	Nor?	(She's) **in** London / **at** her hotel.	
		Machu Picchu?	(It's) **in** Peru.	
		Ryan from?	(He's **from**) Australia.	

A Complete the questions and answers with *who, where, in,* or *at* and information from the chart.

Name	Hometown	Where is he or she now?
Emma ♀	Berlin, Germany	on vacation / Mexico
Hisham ♂	Rabat, Morocco	on vacation / Italy
Jun ♂	Beijing, China	Mei's house
Mei ♀	Beijing, China	home
Tim ♂	Toronto, Canada	work / New York City

1. ___Who___ is from Rabat?   Hisham is.

2. _____'s Rabat?   It's _____ Morocco.

3. Where is Hisham now?   He's _____.

4. _____ is Emma from?   She's _____.

5. Who's _____ the US now?   _____.

6. _____ exactly is Tim?   He's _____ work _____ New York City.

7. Where are Mei and Jun?   They're _____.

8. Who's on vacation now?   _____.

B Write three new *who* or *where* questions about the information in the chart. Ask a partner the questions.

LESSON B

	Be	Adjective	
ADJECTIVES WITH *BE*			
Copacabana	**is**	relaxing.	Adjectives are words that describe nouns.
The penguins	**are**	cute.	Adjectives follow *be*.
Carnival	**is**	fun and loud.	Use *and* to join two adjectives.

	Be	Adjective	Noun	
It	**is**	a popular	place.	Adjectives can come before nouns.
There	**are**	big	stadiums.	Use *a* or *an* before singular nouns.

A Circle the adjectives and underline the nouns.

1. It's a crowded place.
2. Are you a busy person?
3. They are tall and beautiful.
4. She's a friendly teacher.
5. The building is big and old.
6. Our small town is famous for good food.

B Put the words in parentheses into the sentences. Write the new sentences.

1. He's English teacher. (an)

   _____

2. The restaurant is small friendly. (and)

   _____

3. The student is in our class. (new)

   _____

4. It's a city of five million people. (large)

   _____

5. There's a view from the mountain. (wonderful)

   _____

6. It's a big city with the feeling of a town. (small)

   _____

3 POSSESSIONS

LESSON A

<table>
<tr><th colspan="5">SINGULAR AND PLURAL COUNT NOUNS</th></tr>
<tr><td>It's</td><td>an</td><td>ID card.</td><td></td><td rowspan="3">Count nouns are singular (= one thing) or plural (= two or more things).
Use a or an before singular count nouns only.</td></tr>
<tr><td>I'm</td><td>a</td><td>student.</td><td></td></tr>
<tr><td>There are many</td><td></td><td>students</td><td>here.</td></tr>
<tr><td colspan="5">When the singular noun begins with a consonant sound, use a.
When the singular noun begins with a vowel sound, use an.</td></tr>
</table>

<table>
<tr><th colspan="2">SPELLING RULES FOR FORMING PLURAL NOUNS</th></tr>
<tr><td>Most plural nouns are formed by adding s:</td><td>camera → cameras   pen → pens</td></tr>
<tr><td>For nouns ending in a <u>vowel</u> + y add s:
For nouns ending in a <u>consonant</u> + y,
drop the y and add ies:</td><td>boy → boys

dictionary → dictionaries</td></tr>
<tr><td>For nouns ending in a <u>vowel</u> + o add s:
For nouns ending in a <u>consonant</u> + o,
add s with some nouns and es with others:</td><td>radio → radios

photo → photos   potato → potatoes</td></tr>
<tr><td>For nouns ending in ch, sh, ss, or x, add es:</td><td>class → classes</td></tr>
<tr><td>For nouns ending in f / fe, change it to ve + s:</td><td>knife → knives</td></tr>
</table>

A Use the words in the box to complete the sentences. In your notebook, write a sentence with each word. (Use a or an for singular words.) Then practice saying the sentences.

~~address 1~~	city 2	eraser 1	key 2	phone 1	umbrella 1
~~backpack 2~~	dictionary 2	ID card 1	laptop 1	photo 2	watch 2

1. It's ___an address___.   2. They're ___backpacks___.

B Complete the sentences with the singular or plural forms of the nouns in parentheses. Then ask and answer the questions with a partner.

1. What's in your backpack?

   _____ (phone), _____ (laptop), and two _____ (bus pass)

2. What's in your wallet?

   _____ (ID card), two _____ (photo), and two _____ (credit card)

3. What's on your desk?

   three _____ (pen), _____ (eraser), and two _____ (dictionary)

LESSON B

	THIS / THAT / THESE / THOSE	
	Near	**Not near**
Singular	❶ **This is** my ID card. ❶ A: Bill, **this is** my friend Nadia. B: Hi, Nadia. Nice to meet you.	❷ A: Who**'s that** over there? B: **That's** Marie Kondo. ❷ **That's** an expensive watch!
Plural	❸ **These** headphones **are** really good. ❸ A: **These are** my parents. B: It's nice to meet you, Mr. and Mrs. Kim.	❹ A: **Are those** your photos? B: Yes, they are.

❶ Use *this* to talk about a person or a thing near you. Use *this is* on the phone or to introduce a person.

❷ Use *that* to talk about a person or a thing that is not near you.

❸ Use *these* to talk about two or more people or things near you. Use *these* to introduce two or more people.

❹ Use *those* to talk about two or more people or things that are not near you.

A Look at the photos. Complete the sentences with *this*, *that*, *these*, or *those*.

1. Is _____ your photo?

2. Are _____ your keys?

3. A: Who's _____?
   B: My teacher.

4. Eva, _____ is Bill.

5. Are _____ your sunglasses over there?

6. Hello, _____ is Pat.

B Add a follow-up sentence or response to 1–6 in **A**. Then practice the conversations with a partner.

4 ACTIVITIES

LESSON A

THE PRESENT CONTINUOUS: AFFIRMATIVE AND NEGATIVE STATEMENTS		
Subject + be		**Verb + -ing**
I'**m** / You'**re** / He'**s** / She'**s** / We'**re** / They'**re** (not)	**watching**	TV.

The present continuous: subject + *am* / *is* / *are* + verb + *-ing*

Use the present continuous to talk about actions happening right now.
Luis / He **is watching** TV.
Luis / He **is not doing** his homework.

In speaking, use contractions.
He'**s watching** TV.
He'**s not doing** his homework. / He **isn't doing** his homework.

Spelling
watch → *watching*
exercise → *exercising*
shop → *shopping*

YES / NO AND WH- QUESTIONS			
Question Word	**Be**	**Verb + -ing**	**Short Answers**
	Are you		Yes, I am. / No, I'm not.
	Is he	**studying?**	Yes, he is. / No, he's not. / No, he isn't.
	Are they		Yes, they are. / No, they're not. / No, they aren't.
What	are you	**doing?**	(I'**m**) **watching** TV.
	is he		(He'**s**) **watching** TV.
Who	are you	**texting?**	(I'**m texting**) my friend.
	is he		(He'**s texting**) his friend.

A Make sentences with the present continuous. Use contractions when possible.

1. _____*I'm doing*_____ (I / do) my homework right now.

2. _____ (Jon / watch) TV with his friends.

3. _____ (Erika and Martin / study) for a test.

4. _____ (We / use) this book in our English class.

5. _____ (I / not / drink) coffee. This is tea.

6. _____ (He / not shop) for a new laptop. _____ (He / buy) a new phone.

B Complete each conversation. Use contractions when possible.

1. A: _____*Are you studying*_____ (you / study) for the test?

   B: No, _____.

   A: _____*What are you doing*_____ (what / do)?

   B: _____ (watch) TV.

2. A: _____ (Nadia / exercise) at the gym?

   B: No, _____.

   A: _____ (what / do)?

   B: _____ (run) in the park.

3. A: _____ (Oscar and Fiona / go) to school now?

   B: No, _____.

   A: _____ (where / go)?

   B: _____ (go) to a soccer game.

LESSON B

A   Maiko is traveling in Ecuador for a month. Read her email to a friend. Complete the sentences with the present continuous. Use contractions when possible.

Hi Kira,

(1.) _____I'm writing_____ (I / write)

to you from Ecuador. Today,

(2.) _____ (our group / visit)

Quito, the capital city. It's really beautiful.

Right now, (3.) _____ (we / eat)

lunch. The food here is so good!

(4.) _____ (I / enjoy)

this program. This week,

(5.) _____ (we / learn)

about the rainforest and the animals in

Ecuador. (6.) _____ (I / also / use) my Spanish a lot, and that's great.

There's only one bad thing: (7.) _____ (It / rain) a lot these days. But

(8.) _____ (the rain / not / stop) us. We are outside every day.

Well, (9.) _____ (we / leave) the cafe now, so that's all my news for today.

(10.) _____ (you / do) anything fun this month?

Write soon,

Maiko

B   Answer the questions. Write the numbers (1–10) from **A** on the correct line.

Which sentences in **A** are about . . .

1. actions happening right now? _____

2. actions continuing for a period of time in the present? _____

 **FOOD**

LESSON A

THE SIMPLE PRESENT: AFFIRMATIVE STATEMENTS		
Subject pronoun	**Verb**	
I / You / We / They	**eat**	meat.
He / She / It	**eats**	

THE SIMPLE PRESENT: NEGATIVE STATEMENTS				
Subject pronoun	**Do / Does + not**	**Verb**		**Contractions with do**
I / You / We / They	*don't*	**eat**	meat.	*don't = do not*
He / She / It	*doesn't*			*doesn't = does not*

Spelling rules for third person singular (*he, she, it*)

In most cases, add *s* to the base form of the verb: *eat* → *eat**s***

If the base form ends in:
- *s, sh, ch, x,* or *z,* add *es*: *tea**ch*** → *teach**es***
- a consonant + *y,* change the *y* to *i* and add *es*: *stud**y*** → *studi**es***
- a consonant + *o,* add *es*: *g**o*** → *g**oes***   *d**o*** → *d**oes***

ℹ Notice this special spelling rule for the verb *have*:

have → *has*

A Complete the sentences. Use contractions when possible and the simple present forms of the verbs in parentheses.

1. Maria _____ (live) in Mexico City, but her parents _____ (live) in a small town.

   She _____ (speak) Spanish, of course, and she also _____ (study) English.

   She _____ (understand) some French, but she _____ (not / speak) it well.

2. Sarah _____ (teach) at a cooking school. She _____ (finish) at 3:00.

   After school, Sarah _____ (go) from campus to a German restaurant.

   She _____ (work) there.

3. In my family, we _____ (not / use) a fork and knife. We _____ (use) chopsticks.

   We _____ (have) rice every day. My little brother _____ (have) milk every morning.

   My mother _____ (not / drink) milk. She _____ (drink) coffee.

B Write sentences about you and your family. Use item 3 in **A** as a model. Share your sentences with a partner.

_____

_____

_____

_____

_____

_____

LESSON B

THE SIMPLE PRESENT: *YES / NO* QUESTIONS				
Do	Subject	Verb	Short answers	Contractions with *do*
Do	you	like	spicy food?	Yes, I **do**. / No, I don't.	do not = don't
Does	he / she			Yes, he / she **does**. / No, he / she doesn't.	does not = doesn't
Do	you			Yes, we **do**. / No, we don't.	do not = don't
	they			Yes, they **do**. / No, they don't.	

A Complete the questions and answers.

1. ___Do___ you like spicy food?   No, _____.

2. _____ they speak English?   Yes, _____.

3. _____ he have breakfast with his family?   No, _____.

4. _____ we have a test today?   Yes, _____.

5. _____ your mother cook well?   Yes, _____.

6. _____ you and your friend eat lunch together?   No, _____.

B Complete the conversations with *Yes / No* questions and answers. Then practice with a partner.

1. **A:** What are you eating?

   B: Pasta with chocolate sauce.

   A: Really? _____ (it / taste) good?

   B: Yes, _____. _____ (you / want) some?

2. **A:** _____ (you / know) Jamie Oliver?

   B: No, _____. Who is he?

   A: He's a famous chef from England.

   B: Oh yeah! _____ (he / have) a show on TV?

   A: _____. It's on Channel 4.

3. **A:** My parents want to go to a nice restaurant. _____ (you / know) a good place?

   B: _____ (they / like) spicy food?

   A: No, _____.

   B: Oh, okay. Well, _____ (they / eat) sushi?

   A: _____. They love it.

   B: Try Umami Sushi. It's a good place.

C In your notebook, write short answers to the questions. Then compare your answers with a partner's.

1. Do you want to try the pasta with chocolate sauce?

2. Do you know Jamie Oliver or other famous chefs?

3. Do your parents like spicy food? How about sushi? Do you?

6 RELATIONSHIPS

LESSON A

POSSESSIVE NOUNS	
Singular nouns	**Beth's** grandmother is 85.
Plural nouns	Her **sisters'** names are Sonia and Nadia.
Irregular plural nouns	The **men's** names are Carlos and Andres.
Names ending in -*s*	**Carlos's** / **Carlos'** family is from Peru.

A Complete the sentences with a possessive singular or plural noun. Use the word(s) in parentheses.

1. My _____sister's_____ (sister) name is Laura.

2. My _____ (brother) names are Ben and Noah.

3. In your country, what _____ (men) and _____ (women) names are popular?

4. What are your _____ (classmate) names?

5. Tomorrow is _____ (Mother) Day in Japan.

6. _____ (Tomas) family lives in Mexico City.

7. _____ (Mr. Lopez) sons study in the UK.

8. His _____ (son) names are Diego and Martin.

> **WORD BANK**
> son = male child
> daughter = female child

B Write sentences about the things below. Use the possessive.

1. The name of your teacher
   My *teacher's name is* . . .
   _____

2. The names of two classmates
   _____
   _____

3. The name of your friend
   _____
   _____

4. Popular names for men in your country
   _____
   _____

LESSON B

HAVE GOT			
I**'ve** / You**'ve** / We**'ve** / They**'ve**	got	a good job. a nice apartment. a big family. a lot of free time.	I**'ve got** = I **have got** you**'ve got** = you **have got** he's / she**'s got** = he / she **has got** we**'ve got** = we **have got** they**'ve got** = they **have got**
He**'s** / She**'s**			

Have got means the same as *have*. Use *have* or *have got* to talk about:

• things you have or own.
*He **has** / **has got** a good job.*
*She **has** / **has got** a nice apartment.*

• relationships.
*I **have** / **have got** a big family.*

• schedules.
*They **have** / **have got** a lot of free time.*

In speaking, use contractions.
*I**'ve got** a big family.*
*She**'s got** a nice apartment.*

Only use *have* (not *have got*) in these cases:
*I **have** breakfast in the morning. (I've got breakfast . . .)*
*I **have** fun with my friends. (I've got fun . . .)*

A Complete the sentences with *have got* or *has got*.

1. Paolo isn't single. He _____ a girlfriend.

2. I _____ an older sister and a younger brother.

3. Mom isn't home now. She _____ a doctor's appointment today.

4. My sister and I can't go to the party. We _____ a lot of homework.

5. Akemi's parents live in Japan. They _____ a beautiful house there.

6. You _____ six classes this term? Wow, you're busy!

B Read the sentences. Can you use both *have* and *have got*? Or can you only use *have*? Choose the correct answer(s).

1. **A:** Is Linda an only child?

   B: No, she **has** / **'s got** a brother and a sister.

2. **A:** Do you take the bus to school?

   B: No, I **have** / **'ve got** a scooter. I drive to school.

3. **A:** Is there a party at Nina's house?

   B: Yes, she **has** / **'s got** a party for her birthday every year.

4. **A:** I need some money for coffee.

   B: Here, I **have** / **'ve got** $5.

5. **A:** Do you eat lunch at school?

   B: Yes. I **have** / **'ve got** lunch in the school cafeteria.

 **TIME**

LESSON A

PREPOSITIONS OF TIME	

When's your class?
  It's **at** 8:30.
  It's **in** the morning.
  It's **on** Monday.
  It's **from** 4:00 **to** 5:30.
  It's **from** Monday **to** Friday.
	Use *when* to ask about times and days.
	Use *at* for an exact time.
	Use *in* for a period of time.
	Use *on* for days of the week.
	Use *from . . . to* for start and finish times.

ℹ️ *Notice*

in the morning
at night

A Read about Lucia's schedule. Fill in the blanks with *at*, *in*, *on*, *from*, or *to*.

My name is Lucia. I start work (1.) _____ the evening. I start (2.) _____ 9:00 p.m. and finish (3.) _____ 6 a.m. It's hard to work (4.) _____ night.

My husband works (5.) _____ 9 a.m. (6.) _____ 6 p.m. He wakes up (7.) _____ 6 a.m., takes a shower, and eats breakfast. He leaves the house (8.) _____ 8:30. I go to bed then!

I don't work (9.) _____ Saturday. It's my day off. I do some shopping (10.) _____ the morning. My husband and I go to the park (11.) _____ the afternoon.

B Think of a person you know. Write about their work schedule. Complete the chart.

Starting time	
Time of day	
Hours	
Day(s) off	

C Write a few sentences about the person in **B**.

Example

My father starts work at 8:30 in the morning. He works from 8:30 to 6:00.

He's off on Saturday and Sunday.

_____

_____

_____

_____

_____

_____

LESSON B

THE SIMPLE PRESENT: *WH-* QUESTIONS					Short answers
Question word	*Do / Does*	**Subject**	**Main verb**		
Where	**do**	**you**	**go**	on the weekend?	*Where do you go on the weekend?*
		I	go	to the park.	*To the park.*
What	**does**	**she**	**do**	after school?	*The park.*
		She	studies.		
When	**do**	**classes**	**start?**		*Who do you study with?*
		They	start	on Wednesday.	*Hector.*
Who	**do**	**you**	**study**	with?	
		I	study	with Hector.	

A   Read each item. Then use the words in parentheses and information in the responses to complete the questions.

1. **A:** Who _____*do you live*_____ (you) with?

   B: I live with my father, mother, and sister.

2. **A:** When _____ (your mother) in the morning?

   B: She wakes up at 6:15.

3. **A:** Where _____ (your grandparents)?

   B: They live next door.

4. **A:** When _____ (this class)?

   B: It finishes at 4:30.

5. **A:** Where _____ (you) to school?

   B: I go to school at Meiji University.

6. **A:** What _____ (you) on the weekend?

   B: I go out with my friends.

B   With a partner, ask and answer the questions in **A**.

8 SPECIAL OCCASIONS

LESSON A

WH- QUESTIONS WITH PREPOSITIONS	
St. Patrick's Day is <u>on</u> Saturday. **What day is St. Patrick's Day <u>on</u>?** The parade is <u>at</u> 11:00. **What time is the parade <u>at</u>?** I live <u>in</u> Brazil. **What country do you live <u>in</u>?** She lives <u>with</u> her parents. **Who does she live <u>with</u>?** He listens <u>to</u> hip-hop. **What kind of music does he listen <u>to</u>?**	Many sentences have verbs followed by prepositions. When we make question forms for those sentences, the preposition moves to the end of the sentence.

A Unscramble the words to make questions.

1. are / thinking / what / about / you

   _____

2. you / do / from / come / where

   _____

3. who / study / you / with / do

   _____

4. floor / do / live / what / you / on

   _____

5. send / you / do / who / to / emails

   _____

6. do / what / you / city / in / live

   _____

7. of / listen / you / what / to / do / kind / podcasts

   _____

8. which / do / school / to / you / go

   _____

B With a partner, ask and answer the questions in **A**.

LESSON B

When is the Balloon Fiesta?
How long is the Balloon Fiesta?
    It's **from** October 5 **to** October 13.*
 	
When is summer break?
How long is summer break?
    It's **from** July **to** September.
	Use *from . . . to* to answer questions (about dates and seasons) with *when* and *how long*.

When is the Balloon Fiesta?
    It's **in** October. / It's **in** the fall.
    It **in** the early evening. / It's **in** 2021.
	In is used to show <u>a point in time</u>.
	Use *in* before months, seasons, times of day, and years.

How long is the Balloon Fiesta?
    It lasts **for** nine days.
    Nine days.
	For is used to show a <u>period of time</u>.

*Remember: When you read it aloud, say "October fifth to October thirteenth."	

A   Complete the questions with *When* or *How long*. In some cases, both answers are possible.

1. **A:** _____ do you study?

   B: For an hour.

2. **A:** _____ is Independence Day?

   B: It's in the summer.

3. **A:** _____ does this class meet?

   B: It meets from 2:00 to 2:45.

4. **A:** _____ does school start?

   B: It starts in April.

5. **A:** _____ do you prepare for a big test?

   B: For three days.

6. **A:** _____ is winter break?

   B: It's from December 20 to January 10.

7. **A:** _____ is your favorite show on?

   B: In the evening.

B   With a partner, ask and answer the questions in **A**.

9 TOGETHER

LESSON A

FREQUENCY ADVERBS		

with *be*	Emilio <u>is</u> **always** late for class. 100%
	     usually
	     often
	     sometimes
	     hardly ever
	     never 0%
		Frequency adverbs come after the verb *be*. Simple present: Emilio <u>is</u> **never** late for class.
		 Present continuous: Emilio <u>is</u> **always** <u>studying</u>.

with other verbs	Emilio **always** <u>pays</u> his rent on time.	With other verbs, most frequency adverbs come before the main verb.
sometimes* and *usually	**Usually** Emilio takes out the trash. But Adam does it **sometimes**.	***Sometimes*** and ***usually*** can come at the beginning or the end of a sentence.
with *not*	Emilio <u>isn't</u> **usually** late for class. Emilio <u>doesn't</u> **usually** go to bed early. **Sometimes** Emilio <u>doesn't</u> do his chores.	Frequency adverbs come after ***not***, except for ***sometimes***. Don't put ***sometimes*** after ***not***.

A   Unscramble the words to make sentences.

1. hardly ever / make / I / bed / my

   _____ in the morning.

2. makes / bed / my roommate / her / always

   _____

3. is / my roommate / always / working

   _____

4. don't / usually / see / I

   _____ her during the week.

5. watch / sometimes / a movie / my roommate and I

   _____ together.

6. late / are / never / we

   We pay rent on the first of the month. _____

B   Rewrite the sentences with frequency adverbs so they are true for you.

1. I make my bed in the morning.

   _____

2. I'm late for class.

   _____

3. In my house, I make dinner.

   _____

4. At night, I watch TV or play video games.

   _____

5. I wake up early on the weekend.

   _____

LESSON B

REVIEW OF QUESTION FORMS: *BE*				ANSWERS
Wh- word	*Be*	Noun / Pronoun		
Who	's / is	Jessica?		She's Fukue's friend.
Where	's / is	Fukue?		She's in Japan.
	Are	they	old friends?	Yes, they are. No, they aren't. / No, they're not.

REVIEW OF QUESTION FORMS: OTHER VERBS					ANSWERS
Wh- word	*Do*	Noun / Pronoun	Verb		
When	do	you	hang out	with friends?	After school.
How long	does	she	study?		For about an hour.
	Do	you	make	friends easily?	Yes, I do. / No, I don't.

A Read the conversation about a movie. Complete each question.

A: ___*What are*___ you doing?

B: I'm watching a short movie.

A: _____ it called?

B: It's called *Finding Fukue*.

A: _____ it interesting?

B: Yes, it _____.

A: _____ it about?

B: It's about two childhood friends.

A: _____ the two friends' names?

B: Fukue and Jessica.

A: _____ the story take place?

B: In Japan.

A: _____ it take place?

B: In 2018.

A: _____ is the movie?

B: Only about 20 minutes.

A: _____ you like it?

B: Yes, I like it a lot.

B Work with a partner. Think about a movie or TV show about friends. Take turns asking and answering questions about it.

A: I'm watching a drama.

B: What's it called?

A: It's called *Itaewon Class*.

B: I don't know it. Is it popular?

A: Yes, it is.

 **HOME**

LESSON A

THERE IS / THERE ARE				
Singular	There is / There's	an	elevator	in the building.
		no		
Plural	There are	(two)	elevators	
		no		

Use *there is* to say that something exists in a place.

> **There's** <u>an elevator</u> <u>in the building</u>.
>   thing   place

Use *there are* to say that two or more things exist in a place. With the plural, sometimes we don't say the number.

> **There are** <u>two elevators</u> in the building.
> **There are** <u>elevators</u> in the building.

In negative sentences, use *no*.

> **There's** no elevator in the building.
> **There are** no elevators in the building.

Questions				Short Answers
Is there	an elevator		in the building?	Yes, **there is**.
				No, *there isn't.*
Are there (any)	elevators			Yes, **there are**.
				No, *there aren't.*
How many	elevators	are	in the building?	**There's** one.
				There are two.

A Complete the sentences with *there is* (*there's*) or *there are*.

1. _____ one bedroom in the apartment.

2. _____ two closets.

3. _____ large windows in the living room.

4. _____ a nice view from the living room.

5. _____ a kitchen with a refrigerator and a microwave.

B In these sentences, use the negative with *there is* (*there's*) or *there are*.

1. _____ washing machine in the apartment.

2. _____ AC in the bedroom.

3. _____ chairs in the living area.

4. _____ window in the bathroom.

5. _____ restaurants in the area.

C Complete each question and short answer.

1. A: _____ bedrooms are in the apartment?

   B: _____ one.

2. A: _____ a bathtub in the bathroom?

   B: _____. There's a shower only.

3. A: _____ closets are in the apartment?

   B: _____ two.

4. A: _____ stores are in the area?

   B: _____ a lot—over twenty.

LESSON B

VERY AND TOO					
This room	is		**very**	dark.	
He	has	a	**very**	small	apartment.
The desk	is		**too**	big	for the room.
It	is		**too**	hard	to study	in a bright room.

Very and *too* make <u>adjectives</u> stronger.
  *This room is **very** <u>dark</u>.*
  *The desk is **too** <u>big</u> for the room.*

Use *too* to say that something is excessive, with a negative result.
  *The desk is **too** big. It doesn't fit in the room.*
  *The apartment is **too** small for four people. Only two can live there.*

Too + adjective is sometimes followed by an <u>infinitive</u> (*to* + verb).
  *It's **too** hard <u>to study</u> in a bright, white room.*

You can only use *a very* + adjective + noun. Don't use *too*.
  *He has **a very** small apartment.*
  ~~He has a too small apartment.~~

A Complete the sentences with *very* or *too*.

1. It's _____ noisy in here. I can't hear you. Let's go outside.

2. This is a _____ beautiful color. Let's use it in the dining room.

3. These chairs are _____ old, but we can still use them.

4. This dorm room is _____ small for four people. Four students can't live in here.

5. My neighbor is a _____ nice person. I like him a lot.

6. It's _____ cold to study in this room. Let's go to the kitchen.

7. He lives in a _____ large apartment; it's almost 200 square meters!

8. I'm _____ tired to walk to the fifth floor. I'm taking the elevator.

9. The rent here is $1,000 a month. That's _____ expensive for me. I can only pay $800.

10. These apartments are _____ expensive, but a lot of people buy them.

B Complete the sentences with *very* or *too* and your ideas. Then explain your answers to a partner.

1. My bedroom is _____.

2. I'm too old to _____.

3. I'm too young to _____.

4. English is _____.

11 CLOTHING

LESSON A

HAVE TO AND WANT TO			
	Verb / Verb + *to*	**Verb**	**Noun**	
❶ She	**has**		winter boots.	
❷ She	**has to**	wear	four jackets	to go outside.
❸ He	**wants**		a silk scarf.	
❹ He	**wants to**	buy	a gift	for his sister.
❶ Use *have* + noun for things you possess.				
❷ *Have to* + verb has a different meaning. Use it to say that something is necessary.				
❸ Use *want* + noun for things you don't possess (but desire).				
❹ Use *want to* + verb for things you wish to do.				

A Complete the sentences with *to*. If *to* isn't needed, write *X*.

1. I have _____ a test tomorrow. I have _____ study tonight.

2. Does Aya want _____ a new jacket for her birthday?

3. Diego doesn't have _____ wear a suit on Fridays.

4. Cleo wants _____ buy a new dress for the party.

5. I don't have _____ money for the bus. Do you?

6. Martin has _____ English class at 9:00 a.m. He has _____ leave home by 8:00.

7. Do you want _____ see a movie tonight?

8. I want _____ wear a jacket to the party. Do I have _____ wear a tie, too?

B Make the sentences true for you. Complete each one with *(don't) want to* or *(don't) have to*. Share your answers with a partner.

1. I _____ study English.

2. I _____ wear jeans on the weekend.

3. I _____ stay at school every day until 4 p.m.

4. I _____ wear a uniform to school.

5. I _____ buy some new clothes.

LESSON B

English divides nouns into things we can count (count nouns) and things we can't (noncount nouns).

Count nouns are singular (= one thing) and plural (= two or more things). *I have four **ties**, but none of them match this **shirt**.*	**Noncount nouns** only have a singular form. They don't have a plural form. *What kind of **jewelry** do you like?*
Use *a* or *an* before **singular count nouns**. *I need **a** new **jacket** for my interview.*	Don't use *a* or *an* before **noncount nouns**. *I need new **jewelry** for my interview.*
Use *some* for general amounts. Use it with **plural count nouns** only. *I have **some** nice **skirts**.*	Use *some* with **noncount nouns**, too. *I need to buy **some** new **furniture**.*
Use *a pair of* to count things that are always plural (*pants* → *a pair of pants*). You can also use *a pair of* to count things that come in sets of two (*shoes* → *a pair of shoes*).	
Common noncount nouns: *furniture, garbage, jewelry, mail, money, music, vocabulary*	

A Write *a* / *an* or *X*.

1. **A:** Do you wear _____ jewelry?

   B: Only _____ wedding ring.

2. **A:** I need _____ pair of gloves. Let's go shopping.

   B: Sorry, but I have to do _____ homework.

3. **A:** How much _____ money do I need for the bus?

   B: _____ dollar.

4. **A:** Oh, no! It's raining. I don't have _____ jacket.

   B: Don't worry, I always have _____ umbrella in my bag. We can share it.

5. **A:** Do you wear _____ dress clothes to work?

   B: I wear _____ dress shirt, but _____ casual pants—usually _____ pair of jeans.

B Look at the list of items. Complete the task.

1. Which ones can take *a pair of*? Check (✓) your answers.

2. Choose any three words from the list. Write a sentence using each one. Use *a /an*, *a pair of*, *some*, or nothing before each noun.

☐ blouse   ☐ sneakers

☐ clothes   ☐ socks

☐ gloves   ☐ sunglasses

☐ jewelry   ☐ sweater

1. _____

2. _____

3. _____

 **JOBS**

LESSON A

QUESTIONS WITH *LIKE*	
A: I'm a game developer. **B:** Really? **What's** that **like**? **A:** It's fun, but the hours are long.	You can use *like* to ask questions about an experience. In this question, *that* means *being a game developer*.
A: My coworker is from Brazil. **B:** Oh? **What's** he **like**? **A:** He's nice.	You can also use *like* to ask questions about a person and his or her personality. What's *he* like? What are *they* like?

A Complete the conversations with the correct questions.

1. **A:** Ms. Collins is my math teacher this term.

   B: Oh. _____

   A: She's very nice.

2. **A:** I'm a student at Stanford University.

   B: Really? _____

   A: It's a great school. I love it.

3. **A:** My brother works in an office.

   B: _____

   A: Sometimes it's boring, but it's a good job.

4. **A:** We have a new office manager.

   B: Really? _____

   A: He's very organized and helpful.

LESSON B

TALKING ABOUT ABILITY WITH *CAN* / *CAN'T*		
I / You / He / She / We / They	**can** / *can't*	<u>speak</u> French.

Can and *can't* are followed by the <u>base form</u> of the verb.
Can't is the short form of *cannot*. In spoken English, *can't* is more common.

QUESTIONS WITH *CAN* / *CAN'T*		
Yes / **No questions**	**Can** you speak French?	Yes, I **can**. / No, I *can't*.
Wh- questions	Which languages **can** you speak?	(I **can** speak) Spanish and English.
	Who **can** speak Japanese?	Toshi (**can**).

A Complete the conversations with a question or answer with *can* or *can't*.

1. **A:** Can Mario drive?

   B: No, _____. He's only 14.

2. **A:** _____?

   B: Yes, _____. I'm a good driver.

3. **A:** _____?

   B: No. Catia's parents can't speak English.

4. **A:** _____?

   B: Yes. Linda can swim, but her sister _____.

B Make questions and answers about Adam and Sonya using *can* and the words given.

Adam:	musician	Sonya:	software developer
Languages:	English and Mandarin	Languages:	Spanish and English
Hobbies:	I like to ski and play guitar.	Hobbies:	I like to dance and ski.

1. Who / speak Mandarin? _____

   Adam can (speak Mandarin). _____

2. What / languages / Sonya / speak? _____

   _____

3. Who / build / websites? _____

   _____

4. Which / instrument / Adam / play? _____

   _____

5. Who / ski? _____

   _____

UNIT 4: LESSON A, GRAMMAR

B Look at the photo. What are Omar and Alba doing? Write sentences.

C Your partner's photo is similar to yours, but there are some differences. Find the differences together. Ask questions.

> " In your photo, is Omar talking to Alba?
>
> No, he's not. He's . . . "

D Repeat **B** and **C** with this new photo.

UNIT 6: LESSON A, ACTIVE ENGLISH

A **Student A**: Work on your own. Read 1–10 below. Write the answers.

Questions to ask your partner

In English, what's the word for your . . .

1. mother's father? _____

2. father's brother? _____

3. own male child? _____

4. parents' parents? _____

Do the math.

5. What is 25 + 25? _____

6. What is 31 + 44? _____

7. What is 100 – 11? _____

8. What is 70 – 29? _____

Talk about your family.

9. Who is the youngest person in your family? How old is the person?

10. Who is your favorite family member? What is the person's name and how old is he or she?

WORD BANK

+ plus
– minus

oldest
youngest

B Work with your partner. To do this exercise, you need a timer. Follow the steps. If you don't know an answer, say *pass*.

1. One person goes first. Start the timer.

2. Ask your partner your questions in **A** (1–10). Your partner answers quickly.

    Check (✓) the answers your partner says correctly.

3. At the end, write your partner's total time and the number of correct answers.

4. Switch roles and repeat steps 2 and 3.

C Compare your scores. Who did better: you or your partner?

D On your own, create your own quiz of 10 items (like the one in **A**).

E Work with your partner again. Repeat **B** and **C**.

A Work with a partner. Follow these steps.

STUDENT B
- Look at the activities in your schedule below. Don't show your schedule to Student A.
- Task 1: You're taking a big test on Friday afternoon at 4:00. You want to study with your partner for two hours to prepare for the test. Find a good time to study together.
- Task 2: You want to see a movie at 7:00 in the evening. Find a good day to go.

> Discuss your Wednesday schedules first. Then look at your Thursday and Friday schedules.
> Use these expressions: *Are you free ...?*   *I'm busy.*

My schedule

	Wednesday	Thursday	Friday
1:00	eat lunch		
2:00		eat lunch	
3:00	in class		
4:00	in class		take a test
5:00		exercise	work
6:00			work (finishes at 6:15)
7:00	eat dinner		

Student A: Let's study together for the test.

Student B: Good idea!

Student A: Are you free on Wednesday at 3:00?

Student B: I'm sorry, but I'm busy then. I'm in class. How about 5:00?

B Think of your own idea for Saturday or Sunday. Make a plan with your partner.

B **Student A:** You are looking for student housing. Follow these steps:

1. Listen to your partner talk about a place for rent. Take notes below.

2. Ask your partner questions to learn about the apartment's "extras." Use *is there / are there.*

   Put a ✓ or an ✗.

66 Is there a refrigerator?

About the apartment for rent	Extras (✓ = yes ✗ = no)
It's on the . . . _____	____ refrigerator?
_____	____ closets?
_____	____ laundry room in the building?
_____	____ elevator?
_____	

WORD BANK
microwave (oven)
refrigerator
window

C Switch roles. Your partner is looking for student housing.

1. Tell your partner about the apartment below.

2. Answer your partner's questions about the apartment's extras. Use *there is / there are.*

About the apartment for rent	Extras (✓ = yes ✗ = no)
It's on the first floor. There's one big room with a bed, a desk, and a chair. There's also a small kitchen and a bathroom.	✓ washing machine (in the kitchen) ✓ windows (one large) ✗ closets ✗ bathtub in the bathroom (shower only)

D Look at the apartments in **B** and **C**. Do you want to live there? Why or why not?

UNIT 10: LESSON B, GRAMMAR

UNIT 12: LESSON B, ACTIVE ENGLISH

EXERCISE C

7–9 points in . . .	Good jobs for you:
Group 1	teacher, lawyer, journalist
Group 2	software developer, doctor, customer service rep
Group 3	musician, DJ, singer

7–9 points in . . .	Good jobs for you:
Group 4	graphic artist, fashion designer, engineer
Group 5	dancer, athlete, coach
Group 6	diplomat, manager, salesperson

UNIT 2: LESSON A, ACTIVE ENGLISH

EXERCISE A
1. Brasilia
2. Chinese
4. Turkey
5. Mexico
6. Cairo
8. Chile
9. New York City
10. the British royal family
12. Jakarta
14. Germany
15. French and English
16. India
17. Venice
19. Thai
20. Austria
21. Brazil, Colombia, Peru, Bolivia, Venezuela, Ecuador

UNIT 8: LESSON A, SPEAKING

EXERCISE E
1. c 2. b 3. c 4. a

UNIT 9: LESSON B, VOCABULARY

EXERCISE B
98% say they have one or more close friends. **20%** say they have six or more.

87% say they have a good friend at school. **35%** have a good friend who lives far away.

60% say they spend time with their friends online every day.

24% say they meet their friends in person every day.

CREDITS

Illustration: All illustrations are owned by © Cengage.

Cover © Kosuke Wakabayashi; **2–3** (spread) © Laura Morton; **4** (tl) LeoPatrizi/E+/Getty Images, (tc) Jasmin Merdan/Moment/Getty Images; **5** Sandy Huffaker/The New York Time/Redux; **6** Ben Pipe Photography/Cultura/Getty Images; **9** Narong Pimsook/EyeEm/Getty Images; **12** (tl) amriphoto/E+/Getty Images, (tr) Randy Miramontez/Alamy Stock Photo, (cr) Zeferli/iStock/Getty Images; **10–11** (spread) Gerd Ludwig/National Geographic Image Collection; **11** Ciril Jazbec/National Geographic Image Collection; **13** Kevin Mazur/Getty Images Entertainment/Getty Images; **14** Julien Hekimian/Getty Image Entertainment/Getty Images; **15** Fei Yang/Moment/Getty Images; **16–17** (spread) Pgiam/iStock/Getty Images; **18** (tc) Matthias Hangst/Getty Images Sport/Getty Images, (bl1) Roberto Machado Noa/LightRocket/Getty Images, (bl2) Jose A. Bernat Bacete/Moment/Getty Images, (br1) Creative Photo Corner/Shutterstock.com, (br2) NurPhoto/Getty Images; **19** Byelikova Oksana/Shutterstock.com; **20** Sandro Bisaro/Moment/Getty Images; **21** murkalor/Shutterstock.com; **22** (tr1) Jaap2/istock Unreleased/Getty Images, (tr2) Mojito_mak/iStock/Getty Images, (tr3) (tr4) Jaap2/E+/Getty Images, (tr5) (tr6) somchaisom/iStock/Getty Images; **23** Richard Brew/Shutterstock.com; **24–25** (spread) Ben1183/iStock/Getty Images; **24** Ariadne Van Zandbergen/Lonely Planet Images/Getty; **26** Tuul & Bruno Morandi/The Image Bank/Getty Images; **27** eFesenko/Alamy Stock Photo; **28** Pierrick Lemaret/Alamy Stock Photo; **29** San Cristóbal/National Geographic Image Collection; **30–31** (spread) © Glen Mitchell; **32** (tr1) John Kasawa/Shutterstock.com, (tr2) carolgaranda/Shutterstock.com, (tr3) Freedom Life/Shutterstock.com, (c) ozanuysal/Shutterstock.com, (bc) RichLegg/E+/Getty Images; **33** © John Stanmeyer; **34** (tr) Dobo Kristian/Shutterstock.com, (cl) Camilla wisbauer/E+/Getty Images, (c) Don Farrall/DigitalVision/Getty Images, (cr) BK foto/Shutterstock.com; **35** Richard Baker/In Picture/Getty Images; **37** © John Thackwray; **38–39** (spread) Africa Studio/Shutterstock.com; **39** Album/Alamy Stock Photo; **40** Gary Yeowell/Digital Vision/Getty Images; **41** (cl1) (cl2) Jaap2/E+/Getty Images; **43** Cavan Images/Getty Images; **44** worapol sittiphaet/Getty Images; **45** Witthaya Prasongsin/Moment/Getty Images; **46–47** (spread) © Md Tanveer Hassan Rohan; **48** (bl1) andresr/E+/Getty Images, (bl2) d3sign/Moment/Getty Images, (bl3) fizkes/Shutterstock.com, (bc) Hispanolistic/E+/Getty Images, (br1) Dougal Waters/Digital vision/Getty Images, (br2) Tom Werner/Digital vision/Getty Images, (cl) Goran Bogicevic/Shutterstock.com, (cr) DragonImages/Alamy Stock Photo; **49** Jordan Siemens/Stone/Getty Images; **50** Hal Bergman/Moment/Getty Images; **51** (cr) GaudiLab/Shutterstock.com; (bc) fizkes/Shutterstock.com; **52** vgajic/E+/Getty Images; **53** Adam Bronkhorst/Alamy Stock Photo; **56** Odd Andersen/AFP/Getty Images; **54** (spread) © Harvard University News Office; **57** Joel Sartore/National Geographic Image Collection; **59** RudyBalasko/iStock/Getty Images; **60–61** (spread) © Ryan Matthew Smith; **62** (tl) mg7/iStock/Getty Images, (tc) spaxiax/Shutterstock.com, (tr) OlgaMiltsova/iStock/Getty Images Plus/Getty Images, (cl) Olga Nayashkova/Shutterstock.com, (c) fotogal/iStock/Getty Images, (cr) VeselovaElena/iStock/Getty Images, (bl) Darryl Brooks/Shutterstock.com, (bc) Brent Hofacker/Shutterstock.com, (br) Dejan Stanic Micko/Shutterstock.com; **63** Jeff Greenberg/Universal image group/Getty Images; **64** Elena Eryomenko/Shutterstock.com; **65** fcafotodigital/E+/Getty Images; **66** Klaus Vedfelt/Cultura/Getty Images; **67** Lisovskaya Natalia/Shutterstock.com; **68–69** (spread) FatCamera/E+/Getty Images; **70** prmustafa/iStock/Getty Images; **71** TorriPhoto/Moment/Getty Images; **72** Vittorio Caramazza/Alamy Stock Photo; **73** Marvin Zilm (13 Photo)/Redux; **74–75** (spread) Kirsten Luce/The New York Times/Redux; **76** (tl1) Mike Tauber/Getty Images, (tl2) Morsa Images/DigitalVision/Getty Images, (tc1) tirc83/E+/Getty Images, (tc2) Diego Cervo/Shutterstock.com, (tr1) Juanmonino/E+/Getty Images, (tr2) kali9/E+/Getty Images, (cl1) DMEPhotography/iStock/Getty Images, (cl2) JohnnyGreig/E+/Getty Images, (cr1) oliveromg/Shutterstock.com, (cr2) FG Trade/E+/Getty Images; **77** © **Familia** Zapp Family; **78** Tetra Images, LLC/Alamy Stock Photo; **82–83** (spread) © Guillaume Herbaut/Institute; **84** © **Wayne Lawrence**; **85** Robert Recker/The Image Bank/Getty Images; **87** David Guttenfelder/National Geographic Image Collection; **88** Evan Sung/The New York Times/Redux; **90–91** (spread) Fabrizio Verrecchia/Unsplash.com; **92** (tl1) (tl2) (tr1) (tr2) jantima14/Shutterstock.com; **93** NASA; **94** gregobagel/Getty Images; **96** Dan Porges/Archive Photos/Getty Images; **97** Eloi_Omella/E+/Getty Images; **98** (tr) picture alliance/Getty Images, (cl) Tetra Images, LLC/DreamPictures/Alamy Stock Photo, (c) Thomas Barwick/Stone/Getty Images; **99** Delmaine Donson/E+/Getty Images; **100** Reuters/Alamy Stock Photo; **103** Marcos Issa/Bloomberg/Getty Images; **104–105** (spread) © Daniel Kudish; **106** Paul Brown/Alamy Stock Photo; **107** R.M. Nunes/Alamy Stock Photo; **108** Paul Faith/AFP/Getty Images; **109** Aflo Co. Ltd./Alamy Stock Photo; **110** GibsonPictures/E+/Getty Images; **111** © Jim Richardson Photography; **112–113** (spread) lukas bischoff/Alamy Stock Photo; **114** Yaacov Dagan/Alamy Stock Photo; **115** Daniel Knighton/FilmMagic/Getty Images; **116** Jeff J Mitchell/Getty Images News/Getty Images; **117** Douglas MacDonald/Moment/Getty Images; **118–119** (spread) Barcroft Media/Getty Images; **121** Alexander Spatari/Moment/Getty Images; **122** Peter Cade/Stone/Getty Images; **123** Antonio Guillem/Shutterstock.com; **125** McKayla Chandler/Shutterstock.com; **126–127** (spread) Corey Arnold/National Geographic Image Collection; **128** © **Ronald C. Stuart**; **130** Maskot/Getty Images; **131** Thomas Barwick/Stone/Getty Images; **132** Christopher Polk/Shutterstock.com; **134–135** (spread) imageBroker/Alamy Stock Photo; **136** jafara/Shutterstock.com; **137** © Joao Pina; **138** Trong Nguyen/Shutterstock.com; **140** Photographee.eu/Shutterstock.com; **141** Iriana Shiyan/Shutterstock.com; **142–143** (spread) Mint Images/Robert Harding Library; **144** Mike Morgan/The Washington Post/Getty Images; **145** Nikada/E+/Getty Images; **146** Zoonar RF/Getty Images; **147** T.H. Culhane/National Geographic Image Collection; **148–149** (spread) Hannah Morales Reyes/National Geographic Image Collection; **150** XiXinXing/Getty Images; **150** Christopher Malcolm/DigitalVision/Getty Images; **151** Beerpixs/Moment/Getty Images; **152** robertharding/Alamy Stock Photo; **153** Paul Chesley/National Geographic Image Collection; **154** Joaquin Corbalan pastor/Alamy Stock Photo; **155** Per-Anders Pettersson/Getty Images News/Getty Images; **156–157** (spread) PeopleImages/E+/Getty Images; **158** 4x6/iStock/Getty Images; **159** Tuul & Bruno Morandi/DigitalVision/Getty Images; **160** Cordon Press/Alamy Stock Photo; **161** (t) VolodymyrSanych/Shutterstock.com, (bc) Anadolu Agency/Getty Images; **162–163** (spread) Christophe Lepetit/Figarophoto/Redux; **164-165** picture alliance/Getty Images; **166** Mark Andrews/Alamy Stock Photo; **167** © **Tran Tuan Viet**; **168** Allies Interactive/Shutterstock.com; **169** Peter Dazeley/The Image Bank/Getty Images; **170–171** (spread) Lutz Jaekel/laif/Redux; **172** dePablo/Zurita/laif/Redux; **173** Jeff Greenberg/Universal Images Group/Getty Images; **175** Corey Arnold/National Geographic Image Collection; **176** STR/AFP/Getty Images; **189** (cl) Erik Isakson/Blend Images/Alamy Stock Photo, (cr) Jamie Carroll/iStock/Getty Images Plus/Getty Images; **193** (cl) Goran Bogicevic/Shutterstock.com, (c) Mika Images/Alamy Stock Photo, (cr) iStock.com/Ababsolutum, (bl) Konstantin Chagin/Shutterstock.com, (bc) hans.slegers/Shutterstock.com, (br) fizkes/Shutterstock.com; **195** Elena Kalistratova/Vetta/Getty Images; **212** (t) GaudiLab/Shutterstock.com, (b) fizkes/Shutterstock.com; **216** (tl) Natalia Kashina/Shutterstock.com, (tr) Mark Kolbe/Getty Images, (cl) Mint Images/Getty Images, (cr) Anthony Asael/Art in All of Us/Getty Images.